AN ANXIOUS KIND OF MIND

A True Story of Rising Above Anxiety Disorders

Randy Fishell

SBC BOOKS

Scriptures credited to NIV are taken from THE HOLY BI-
BLE, NEW INTERNATIONAL VERSION®, NIV® Copyright © 1973, 1978, 1984, 2011 by Biblica, Inc.® Used by
permission. All rights reserved worldwide.

A Couple of Notes to the Reader:

This book is not intended as a substitute for the medical
advice of physicians or other health professionals. The
reader should regularly consult a physician in matters
relating to his/her health and particularly with respect to any
symptoms that may require diagnosis or medical attention.
Neither the author nor publisher shall be liable or responsible
for any health, welfare, or subsequent damage allegedly
arising from the information contained in this book.

Also, I have tried to recreate events, locales, and
conversations from my memories of them. In order to
maintain their anonymity, in some instances I have changed
the names of individuals and places. In addition, I may have
changed some identifying characteristics and details such as
physical properties, occupations, and places of residence.

CONTENTS

PREFACE

Seated on Oahu's North Shore, I marveled as a couple of sea turtles performed their underwater antics. Slanting sun rays backlit each wave, resulting in a translucent, literal sea-foam green color. The awesome creatures rode the currents, frolicking in the warm Hawaiian ocean waters. Were they really as carefree as they looked from my vantage point on the shoreline? Since I have no expertise in sea turtle behavior, I can't give a definitive answer. But they sure looked as if they were having fun, and that's the story I'm sticking with.

For some thirty years, I longed for the kind of freedom and joy those sea turtles appeared to possess. Truth be told, there was a time when the very idea that I'd be spending time so far away from home and actually enjoying it would've seemed ludicrous. Back then, anxiety disorders held me in a stranglehold. Panic attacks, agoraphobia, and obsessive-compulsive disorder (OCD) all appeared uninvited on the stage of my life. In case you aren't familiar with agoraphobia, it's the mental dysfunction that often leaves its victims housebound. Any attempt to leave "safe" and familiar territory brings on anguishing panic symptoms. Although I never became totally housebound, agoraphobia did leave me unable to travel very far alone. I'm not talking about venturing out of the country, or even out-of-state. My phobic behavior would ultimately trigger panic symptoms if I had to drive alone more than about *three blocks* from home. To say that I had a deep mental pit from which to extricate myself would be a world-class understatement.

Actually, the sea turtle episode took place on my *second* business trip (yes, it really was a business trip) to Hawaii. By then, I'd accepted speaking and workshop appointments all across the nation. So just how did I eventually manage to travel thousands of miles from my home in Maryland to Hawaii, plop down on one of its awesome beaches, and love every moment of the experience? In my case, it was preceded by decades of struggle and disappointment. But when I eventually rose above anxiety disorders, I felt like a bashful sea turtle who'd just discovered the thrill of fully embracing that which he was meant to do all along.

Up until the time I put anxiety disorders in their proper place, instead of riding life's waves, they kept beating me back, until I nearly drowned in despair. Anxiety disorders can do that, you know. Most people can't simply talk themselves into mental wellness, at least, I couldn't. You may have tried to do just that, and I commend you for your effort. And lest I be misunderstood, the right kind of self-talk can be immensely helpful on your journey toward rising above anxiety disorders. But when confronting our anxious demons, plenty of us mortals need a little more to roll with than merely hearing our own voice.

The reason I wrote this book is to show you what worked for me as I finally breached the entrapping boundaries of my anxiety-ridden mind. My deep hope is that you clearly understand that your own suffering from anxiety disorders can soon come to an end. You don't have to endure mental agony for decades as I did.

In *An Anxious Kind of Mind*, I give extra attention to the inextricable blending of physical, mental, and other cognitive and behavioral components inherent to anxiety disorders. (It's a lot more complicated than you might think.) This information can open important new vistas as you take stock of your own anxiety challenges.

I am not so naïve as to propose that what worked for me will work for everyone else. What I offer is hard-earned wisdom and guidance to help you choose your own unique path as you push back on anxiety. You really can reclaim your life and do things and go places you once thought impossible.

I would be remiss not to mention that anxiety disorders are far from being fully understood in clinical circles. Its various manifestations—panic, anxiety, depression, obsessive-compulsive disorder, and more—are too intertwined to provide one simple definition. This is confirmed by the multiple diagnoses found in the *Diagnostic and Statistical Manual of Mental Disorders* (*DSM*), the standard classification of mental disorders used by mental health professionals in the United States. I view these various diagnostic categories as a good thing. They allow researchers and therapists to research and provide care on a more personalized basis. Progress is being made, and new avenues of hope are constantly being explored.

What follows is an account of the rise and fall of panic attacks, agoraphobia, and OCD in my life. In writing this book, I've tried to be realistic. Since I'm not a health-care professional, it would be irresponsible to promise a cure. That's not to say it can't or won't happen for you. But most importantly, I share from the vantage point of someone who's actually experienced anxiety's debilitating fallout. While my experience may not be exactly the same as yours, I know firsthand the anguish that can lead someone to question whether anxiety disorders can ever be overcome. I'm here to tell you they can, and to help point you in the right direction and take the first steps toward a brighter tomorrow.

An Anxious Kind of Mind is the story of how my life turned around when the proper pieces of the healing puzzle finally fell into place. Learning what worked for me—and what didn't—may help to save years of futility in *your* search for healing. No, I haven't plastered guarantees of total cure on the covers of this book, and that may rub some readers the wrong way. All I can tell you is the story of how my life was rescued from the deadly shoals of anxiety disorders. While my story is not your story, we can learn from one another. I do think this book can be pivotal in taking you places—figuratively and literally—where you never thought you'd go, either again or for the first time. If my work plays some role in helping you to disallow anxiety disorders unrestricted access to your personhood, a celebration is in order.

May *An Anxious Kind of Mind* provide insight and inspiration as you launch into an exciting life in which anxiety disorders play an ever-diminishing role.

—Randy Fishell

ONE

PANIC ON THE SOUTH SIDE

Dan Ryan is a legendary name for at least a couple generations of Chicago residents. They even named a freeway after the former Cook County Board of Commissioners president.

During the summer of 1973, the Dan Ryan Expressway became for me the shortest route between two critical points. Point A was Berrien Springs—a small village in southwestern Michigan that sits high on a bluff above the adjacent St. Joseph River. My hometown still boasts such beloved establishments as Topper's Bar and Grill, Nikki's Café, and Village Do-It-Best Hardware, where you can get a free bag of popcorn.

Point B was Milton Junction, Wisconsin, where a lovely, brown-eyed teenage farmer's daughter awaited my arrival. I'd been one of Sarah's classmates during my brief stint at a religious boarding high school in Columbus, Wisconsin. Now almost every weekend I tossed a battered suitcase into a vehicle and headed for Sarah's house. I use the generic term *vehicle* instead of *my car,* because circumstances caused this to vary. Sometimes I'd slip into the seat of my bald-tired, gas-guzzling 1961 Lincoln Continental for the trip. But at other times my parents allowed me to take one of their two vehicles, my preference being Mom's new 1973 Plymouth Duster. This little six-cylinder jewel had an added feature: under-dash air-conditioning, a real luxury in those days. In retrospect, this gesture from my parents to their unfocused teenage son likely stemmed from one of two motivations: unconditional parental love or a desire to avoid funeral expenses as the result of my Lincoln skidding broadside on wet pavement into an overpass support pillar.

The only problem with going to Sarah's place on Fridays was that Sundays always loomed just around the corner. That's when I'd need to head south by southeast and roll down the interstate back to Michigan. By this time I'd found a few short-term jobs. My goal was to earn at least enough gas money to head back to Milton Junction on Friday, then back to Michigan on Sunday, repeating the cycle as often as possible.

The return trip from Wisconsin took me down Interstate 294 through Rockford, Illinois, toward Chicago, where I could take one of several routes through the Windy City. From there I'd head around the bottom of Lake Michigan toward Berrien Springs. The entire one-way trip was about 200 miles.

But one Sunday everything changed.

That particular afternoon did not deviate from most July days in greater Chicagoland. The temperature was in the mid-90s, with humidity to match. I'd chosen the Dan Ryan Expressway for this part of the journey. As usual, traffic was bumper-to-bumper, stop and go.

It had been a rough weekend. Sarah and I were having problems, and I'd left her house with romantic issues still unresolved. More accurately, things were a stress-inducing mess, and just the night before I'd experienced some troubling physical symptoms.

"I think you should take me to the emergency room," I'd told Sarah. My constricted chest housed an increasingly rapid heartbeat, and it had become increasingly difficult to take in a deep breath. Adding to the disconcerting physical sensations was a creeping, indefinable sense of foreboding. Something awful—probably even life threatening—was happening to my body and mind. Temporarily setting aside our relational challenges, Sarah grabbed the keys to her dark green Pontiac Lemans and whisked her shaky boyfriend off to the Janesville Hospital emergency room.

The news was not good: the doctor couldn't find anything wrong with me. I wanted more than that! If I were going to endure such disconcerting symptoms, I wanted a genuine diagnosis of doom. But there was no talk of a heart attack, brain tumor, or long-hidden congenital defect.

Instead, the physician on duty seemed pretty casual about the whole thing. "From what you've told me, I'd say you probably had some kind of anxiety issue," he assessed. "A sedative should help you feel better."

I gave my consent, and soon a nurse arrived. I watched as vial and syringe were hoisted toward the overhead fluorescent lights. After filling the device to the appropriate level, she stuck the needle into my arm and delivered the goods. With the calm-inducing medication coursing through my veins, it wasn't long before the doctor's prophecy came true. How could one little shot make such a difference? A few minutes later, I was checked out of the emergency room, and Sarah chauffeured me back to her house. I slept well, hoping this would be the last time I'd experience such unwelcome and intense physical and mental sensations.

But any hope that the unsettling episode would not recur had disappeared by the following afternoon. Trapped in traffic on the Dan Ryan Expressway, I could again tell that something wasn't right. The same set of disturbing symptoms crept over me. But this time, not only was it hard to breathe, my palms grew sweaty, and my hands started tingling. *The heat and humidity must be getting to me,* I reasoned. Thankfully, I was driving Mom's Duster that weekend, so I turned the under-dash air-conditioning unit to its highest setting and pointed its vents toward my face. But the more air I tried to suck in, the worse my symptoms became. I began to feel increasingly dizzy.

Get to an emergency room! my mind screamed. Fat chance. Here I was, stuck in a traffic jam on a freeway in an unfamiliar neighborhood on Chicago's South Side. I had no idea whether a pile of twisted vehicles miles ahead was causing the backup or if this was simply another case of unpredictable Windy City gridlock that might break loose any second. Either way, with affordable GPS and smartphones still decades in the future, I had no way of knowing how far away help might be found.

I was trapped, a reality that wreaked further havoc on my overloaded brain and trembling body. That's when the truth rolled over me like the Mack truck hugging my rear bumper: *I'm going to die right here, right now, on the Dan Ryan Expressway.*

With the air-conditioner still blasting away, I rolled down the car windows. After all, my lungs were crying out for more oxygen, weren't they? But my physical symptoms and mental anguish just kept growing worse. I'd grown up having been taught in both private school and during weekly church services that silent prayer could help at such times. At last an exit sign came into view. I sailed down the Jackson Park off-ramp and began scouting for a possible source of help. Typically, two gigantic golden arches don't signal an urgent care center, but it was the best this stretch of urban streetscape had to offer. I yanked my steering wheel to the right and pulled into the parking lot. Opening my car door, I leaped out and rushed across the pavement and into the fast-food restaurant. Maybe I'd get lucky, and the store associate taking burger orders would be a temporarily out-of-work emergency medical technician.

For whatever reason—maybe the locals were at White Sox Park or home watching the game on TV—it was a slow day at the McBurger joint. I wasted no time in presenting myself at the counter. The teen male store associate began to parrot the standard greeting. "Welcome to—"

"I need you to take me to the hospital," I interrupted.

The poor fellow looked at me uncertainly and said, "What?"

"Look, I'm really sick, and I can't drive my car." I was serious; my increasing lightheadedness had left me unsure how much longer I could safely stay behind the wheel. "I need you to drive me to an emergency room."

I envisioned the young man leaping across the counter

like a Navy SEAL and dragging me out the door toward my car. Instead, he simply said, "I can't leave here."

Of course he was right—I was on my own. "Yeah, OK. So where's the closest hospital?" I asked.

"There's one in that direction," he said, pointing up the street.

I retreated out the door. Pulling out of the parking lot, I hoped the green-light gods would smile upon me. As it turned out, another force was about to appear on the scene.

Chicago's South Side has never been confused with a gun-free zone. Balladeer Jim Croce once paid tribute to one of its renowned residents, albeit a fictional character. Leroy Brown was said to be the "baddest man" around and "meaner than a junkyard dog." The area has improved somewhat since the 1970s, but at the time poverty was pervasive. Predictably, all manner of illicit activities ran rampant throughout the area. That explained why a Chicago police vehicle happened to be cruising toward me.

I stopped my car in the middle of the street, stepped out, and flagged it down. Its flashing light came on as it rolled to a stop. Two officers stepped out and walked up to me. "What's the problem here?" one of them asked.

"Something's wrong with me," I explained. "I'm dizzy and I can't breathe very well. I need to get to a hospital."

Previous to that day I'd never had occasion to converse with a Chicago police officer, but all these years later I still recall their professional, caring demeanor. Still, the lead officer was obliged to ask an obvious question. "Have you been doing any kind of drugs?"

"No, I haven't," I assured him. "I don't know what's happening to me, but I need help—quick." Same as the previous night, I was certain that a critical heart or brain issue was about to claim my life.

The officer asked to see my driver's license. After studying it, he said, "OK, get in my patrol car. Give your car keys to the other officer, and he'll follow us to the hospital in your vehicle.

I did as instructed, and just like that our two-vehicle entourage was speeding toward the Jackson Park Hospital emergency entrance. Upon our arrival the two officers helped to get me checked in. "I'm putting your wallet and car keys in this bag," one officer informed me. "Your car is in the parking lot outside this entrance." He did all this with great specificity, apparently following departmental protocol to the letter.

"Good luck," the other officer said to me. With that, both Good Samaritans made their way toward the exit and disappeared in the twilight.

The personnel on duty seemed to take my situation seriously—for a while. After completing the check-in process and describing my symptoms in detail, I was shown to a vacant gurney and asked to lie down on it. From there I was wheeled into what resembled an indoor parking lot. But instead of vehicles, it housed a colorful cast of beleaguered and bedeviled patients awaiting treatment.

The South Side's population is heavily comprised of African-Americans. As a White person, I was catching a glimpse of life on "the other side of the tracks." Ironically, the South Shore commuter rail line operated just a few miles away. This electric-powered trolley connected rough-and-tumble Chicago with more genteel locales, including South Bend, Indiana, home to Notre Dame University and St. Mary's College. Academics and others

[*15*]

could board the South Shore in the morning, attend business meetings or do research in Chicago all day long, and still make it home in time for a late supper. I wondered if anyone lying on the gurneys to my left and right had ever ridden the train situated near their own back yards.

Over half an hour had passed, when a nurse finally walked over to my gurney and stood near my head. "So you're not feeling too well," she said with a caring smile. "What's going on?" Oddly, by now the worst of the physical symptoms had diminished, but I felt frighteningly alone, even abandoned—but by whom? It made no sense to me. Why, less than a year earlier I'd hitchhiked solo throughout a major portion of the southern United States! If I wasn't scared standing by a road in Florida with my thumb outstretched, why did I now feel such fear of being separated from familiar faces and even places?

After hearing me describe the horrific ordeal I'd just been through, the nurse didn't seem compelled to sound any alarms. "A doctor will stop by and see you in a little while," she announced. With that, she left.

The ebb and flow of fear washed over me. Newly arriving patients temporarily distracted me, relieving my anxiety. But my mind wandered back to my own frightening symptoms, the very act of which made them worse. The sterile overhead fluorescent lights and steady purring of the air conditioning provided a calming effect—until the next siren sounded outside on the streets surrounding the massive old building.

That's when a vague idea resurfaced—a kind of mental trickery I'd employed before with some success. *Somehow I need to get a familiar face to show up here,* I thought. *Then I'd know everything was going to be*

[*16*]

OK. It didn't take long for me to figure out how to make it happen. "Excuse me," I called to the nurse. "Do you think I could make a phone call?"

The nurse hesitated; then said, "Well, I suppose so. I'll show you where there's a phone."

Julie and Marta were two female friends from Michigan attending nursing school in the Chicago suburb of Hinsdale, Illinois. Maybe, just maybe, one or both of them would be willing to come to my aid. Dialing the nursing school phone number, I asked to be transferred to their student housing. A smile crossed my face when I heard a familiar voice on the other end of the line.

"Hey there, Julie, this is Randy. Look, this is kind of weird, but is there any chance you could drive down to the Jackson Park Hospital? I'm here and something kind of strange is going on."

Julie wasn't thrilled with the prospect of coming to see me. She did her best to twist out of responding to my request. "Honestly, with the Sunday night traffic it would take me at least half an hour to get there," she said with evident reluctance. Driving to the crime-ridden South Side of Chicago after nightfall surely was an added disincentive. Nevertheless, after further persuasion, Julie agreed that she and Marta would make the urban trek from Hinsdale to Jackson Park.

What had I done? Why would I urge two busy nursing students to make such an ill-advised trip? Why did I somehow sense that all would be well if only a familiar face arrived on the scene? Shame washed over me—an emotion with which I would grow increasingly intimate.

At last, a doctor appeared. I uttered my symptomatic spiel and awaited his pronouncement.

[*17*]

"Well, it sounds like you had a panic episode," he informed me. "A sedative should help for now."

Here we go again, I thought. While I was in favor of quick relief through chemical intervention, I remained dismayed at the lack of a definitive diagnosis. *What is it going to take for someone to realize there's something terribly wrong with me?* I wondered. Still, I welcomed the relaxing sensation the doctor's prescription soon provided. Maybe I wasn't so alone after all—I'd found a new friend in pharmaceuticals.

About an hour later, Julie and Marta arrived; the traffic had been even worse than anticipated. By then, the Valium-induced calm had taken effect. Still, it was good to have friends close at hand. My conversation with them was veiled and awkward, although I explained some of my symptoms. "I sure hope this doesn't happen again," I said apprehensively.

Julie and Marta didn't quite know how to respond, although as nurses-in-training, they may have determined that my symptoms more closely resembled temporary anxiety than terminal cancer.

Still unused to the sedative's effects, I decided it would be foolish to try and drive the remaining eighty-five miles home to Michigan. Besides, what had happened to me in Wisconsin the night before and in Chicago the following day might happen again. Somehow that thought rattled me. I simply couldn't risk it. Another phone call would bring my parents to the rescue. Although we'd never had a particularly close relationship they, too, were familiar faces, and I welcomed their appearance when they walked into the hospital an hour and a half later. Mom would drive while I slept in the back seat and Dad would follow behind in the other car.

Feeling sheepish and more than a little embarrassed, I thanked Julie and Marta for making the journey. Outside my range of hearing, they spoke briefly with Mom and Dad, then left. As I walked with my parents toward the two family vehicles situated in the hospital's dimly lit parking lot, I had no idea that the downward spiral of living with panic had only begun.

One resource defines panic this way:

> Panic is a sudden sensation of fear so strong as to dominate or prevent reason or logical thinking, replacing it with overwhelming feelings of anxiety and frantic agitation consistent with an animalistic fight-or-flight reaction.[1]

In other words, what happened to me on the Dan Ryan Expressway.

Mark Sichel, a licensed clinical social worker, provides this helpful extrapolation:

> Many child development experts believe that early infancy can be a very scary time. Just imagine a 3-year-old playing in a sandbox, weighing about 40 pounds. He looks up and, instead of seeing his mother, can only—even for a moment—see other children and frightening adults all around him. Translate the weight difference into adult terms: for a tantamount experience you would have to be surrounded by a throng of beings who weighed 700 pounds each and stood 4 times as tall as you. That's

[*19*]

exactly how minor dangers are perceived during a panic attack.[2]

The word *panic* refers to Pan, the Greek god of the woodlands. Apparently, a chief form of entertainment for this dastardly fellow was making spooky sounds that scared the bejeebers out of unsuspecting passersby.[3]

To earn the official title of panic attack, evaluators look for at least four concurrent symptoms. These include heart palpitations, dizziness, shortness of breath, feelings of unreality, and several other such physically- and mentally-anguishing characteristics.[4] I am on a first-name basis with many of these unwelcome intruders.

As in my case, most people experiencing their first panic attack believe they are having a heart attack, or perhaps a nervous breakdown. What's actually going on is that, whatever the trigger, the body's parasympathetic nervous system is throttling up its "fight or flight" protocols. The main fuel for all this activity is epinephrine, otherwise known as adrenaline.

This is good news in an actual emergency situation. Adrenaline provides needed alertness and energy to deal with a genuine threat. But in the case of a panic attack, there is no real emergency or threat. Unfortunately, the panic victim's brain has a mind of its own, and it chooses to bypass rational thought during the event. Surging biochemicals push the thought and body processes in the direction of a worst-case scenario. This intra-psychic alert system can be a godsend when spotting a hulking shadow in a dark alley. We are suddenly prepared to fight or flee, whichever seems more likely to preserve our life. But in the absence of a crisis on which to focus its energy, panic tends to become the threat itself.

Understanding the etiology of panic may be useful, but it's usually not enough to stave off a panic attack. A brain convinced against its will is of the same opinion still, and my brain was deeply persuaded that I must start avoiding any situation that might trigger such mental and physical agony. This meant always being within reasonable proximity of someone who would understand and help me if the worst occurred.

If my life were a canvas, panic would be just one stroke of a highly complex psychodynamic and biochemical painting. Among the paints on my messy mental palette lies an ample squirt of twisted genes. They began to affect my behavior early on. It all began with an African princess and a white crocodile.

.

TWO

OVER AND OVER

Torture chamber would not be too strong a term for what my bedroom had become that Saturday night. The dastardly instrument inflicting pain was a book titled *Nyla and the White Crocodile*.

As a 9-year-old boy, reading in general held little appeal to me. There were a few exceptions, including a series featuring two crime-fighting brothers whose hair-raising adventures had been captured in *The Hardy Boys* series. But its intriguing volumes had remained untouched on my bookshelf for a while now. I had a more important mystery to solve: how to finish a required reading assignment before the end of the school year.

On this Saturday night, I could hear the muffled sound of the *Secret Agent* theme song emanating from the black-and-white television beneath my second-floor bedroom. "There's a man who leads a life of danger, to everyone he meets he stays a stranger . . . "sang Johnny Rivers of secret agent John Drake. How I longed to sport a wrist-mounted walkie–talkie like that worn by the suave British spy guy, played by Patrick McGoohan. But thoughts of international espionage would have to take a back seat tonight.

In the quest to complete my third-grade reading requirements, I'd chosen the book *Nyla and the White Crocodile*. A true story set on the island of Borneo, the book's main character is Nyla, the daughter of Ladah, a village chief. In the book, evil spirits and curses run rampant in the area. The action picks up even further when a white crocodile suddenly appears in the stream below the village and begins licking its chops. The witch doctor on call announces that in order for things to return to normal, a sacrifice must be made to the white crocodile. You guessed it: Nyla is chosen for the honor. About this time, a Christian teacher, Poojee, steps up and challenges the witch doctor to a spiritual duel of sorts. Later, when Nyla disappears under water, it looks like Poojee is on the ropes. But his faith wavers not, and a short time later, Nyla reappears, apparently no worse for the wear. The local tribesmen are convinced the witch's doctor's prescription should be disregarded, a development for which Nyla is indeed thankful.

At the time, I was attending a small school associated with our just-as-small local church. Regarding our reading requirements, our well-intentioned teacher had made it clear that "God would not be pleased" if we wrote down that we'd read something that we actually *hadn't* read. That's all it took for my hypersensitive conscience to kick into overdrive. The book isn't long, but that night of decades past seemed interminable. With the book resting on my knees and my head propped on my pillow, I struggled to get through just one page.

"Nyla walked down to the river that morning." The

sentence was simple enough. But that night something happened in my mind. An unwelcome, silent overseer told me I might not have completely understood what the author meant. How could I honestly say that I'd read the sentence if I hadn't actually totally understood what I'd read? Sure, I'd *seen* the words on the page, but had I actually *understood* them? Maybe not. Then the invisible taskmaster upped the ante. *If you don't want God to be mad at you, you'd better read each sentence until you understand it.*

So I did. Against my will, late into the night I read every sentence over and over until at last I could no longer fight the long tentacles of sleep reaching down to claim me. With a tear slipping down my cheek, I lay the book on my nightstand and turned out the light. For all the agony I'd just been through, I'd read perhaps half a dozen pages.

I hated Nyla and that stupid white crocodile.

My experience with *Nyla and the White Crocodile* was an early manifestation of obsessive-compulsive disorder. Technically speaking, OCD is no longer categorized as an anxiety disorder in the current edition (fifth) of the *Diagnostic and Statistical Manual for Mental Disorders*, the manual published by the American Psychiatric Association that lists all classifications of mental disorders. If you're suffering from anxiety disorders in some fashion, do not feel that your bevy of symptoms *must* include OCD! But because it is so inextricably intertwined with my anxiety disorders experiences, I feel that I would be remiss to not mention it in this book.

So just what kind of person *may* find himself or herself susceptible to OCD? Like those villagers in Nyla's village, did my adolescent interest in being a sincere God-follower make me unreasonably conscientious? Had a curse been placed on me, either by some evil entity, or by a classmate who simply wanted to finish her reading requirements before I did? Or was there perhaps another explanation, one that didn't involve demons or voodoo dolls?

As it turns out, the answer to what exactly tilts a person in the direction of an anxiety disorder depends on whom you ask. Many experts agree that anxiety happens due to a combination of biology and psychology. Researchers believe that some people have a biological vulnerability, such as an overactive nervous system, that makes them more prone to anxiety. It's no different than the way you inherit other characteristics, such as weight and hair color.

Leonard Fishell, grandfather on my father's side, was a man of many talents. History's arc of self-autonomy was not in his favor, however. Leonard was struggling to raise a family during the depression era, which meant that selling his detailed landscape paintings was about as likely as Herbert Hoover himself stopping by to choose one for the East Room.

I still harbor a vague visual memory of Grandpa Fishell's attic studio in my hometown of Berrien Springs, Michigan, where he and his wife, Margaret (Taylor), my grandmother, had moved during their later years. In reality, the studio consisted of little more than an easel and a few tubes of paint scattered about. His landscape painting that today hangs in our home's sunroom was apparently not created in this studio, however. Underneath his signature on the back of the painting, Leonard wrote the words "Allegan, Michigan." That's where he and Margaret had first settled down to raise a family. Their efforts would eventually result in a daughter, Edith, and my father, Martin, both of whom ultimately took up accounting as a profession.

I will dramatically understate the case and simply say that Leonard was not a party animal. Looking back, I can see with relative (no pun intended) clarity that my grandfather suffered from a mental illness. Not Jekyll and Hyde schizophrenia or Green River Killer sociopathic inclinations. Rather, I suspect he was a lot like me. While my wife's energy level skyrockets at social gatherings, it takes me a week to recover from such events. This has nothing to do with drinking too many martinis or consuming off-brand caviar, neither substance of which I partake. It's due to the exhaustion of pretending I am actually enjoying the party. (Maybe I *should* take up martini-drinking—it might make things easier!)

Admittedly, this problematic behavior frequently crosses the line from discomfort to some level of dysfunction. What's behind this bent toward reclusiveness? Some therapists believe that at least some of this may be acquired through family, whether through genes or learning to absorb the anxiety from a family member or members. Whatever its root cause, it is physically and emotionally draining.

I refer to this preference for solitude as "problematic" because it often makes me look anti-social. Prime example: people cannot understand why I refuse to play the card game *Pit* when my wife yells and trades grain cards late into the night until at last she drops from exhaustion. My preference to not join in the melee results in a socially awkward situation, a.k.a., "problematic." Don't get the wrong idea; I don't lock myself in the closet every New Year's Eve. It just means that I know what to expect and that I am wise to head for home before the gang launches into "Auld Lang Syne."

As for Leonard, it's hard to pinpoint exactly when his troubles began. I do know that shortly after getting married, the man set out solo from Michigan for North Dakota, where the soil was richer and the land cheaper to rent. My grandfather was determined to prove his family provider mettle, and wheat was his crop of choice.

Upon seeing the first sprouts breaking through the fertile soil, Leonard must have shouted "Yesss!" and leaped for joy. No, wait, more likely he gave a faint nod of approval when nobody was looking. Whatever his reaction, the plants thrived—that is, until a legendary hailstorm destroyed the entire crop, and along with it, my grandfather's dream of financial independence. Later, during the Great Depression, back in Michigan he could be seen peddling turnips door-to-door, trying to scrape up enough cash to purchase some cornmeal and another packet of cigarettes.

The landscape painting in my sunroom does not give any written indication of its setting; it appears to be somewhere on the Great Plains. The clouds are gray, and the hills are covered in snow. In the foreground is a small homestead comprised of a cabin and barn, with a stream nearby. Is this my grandfather's dream captured on canvas? Are Leonard and Margaret inside the cabin, quietly celebrating their bountiful wheat crop while warming themselves by the fire as the cold North Dakota wind swirls around them?

Only much later did my late father share with me a few more details about his own father's mental health. Dad told me about the time he'd recently been discharged from World War II military service after having served as a medic onboard the U.S.S. *Queen Mary*. One of his first duties upon reentering civilian life involved another discharge, that of securing his father's release from the mental institution in Kalamazoo, Michigan, where he'd been placed.

I do not believe my grandfather was a bona fide "mental case;" certainly not in the sense that the term has come to be understood in popular culture. Looking back, though, I do see a few puzzle pieces that have at last begun to find their proper places.

Growing up, I'd always found it a little odd that Leonard had never gotten a driver's license. At least, if he possessed one, I never saw him use it to get behind the wheel. On the rare occasions when he did leave the house and found it necessary to travel beyond walking distance, my grandmother was always the designated driver. My dad's sister, Edith, along with her husband, Everett, and their two children, still lived in Allegan, about sixty-five miles north of Berrien Springs. Years later, my cousin Doug recalled at least one occasion when our grandparents traveled in their red 1956 Ford Victoria to visit the relatives. Upon their arrival, Leonard refused to leave the car. Instead, any interaction between grandfather and grandchildren (or any of the other family members, for that matter) took place on the passenger side of the automobile. The whole arrangement resembled that of a prison inmate visitation session. My grandmother was hardly a community socialite, but surely such behavior on the part of her husband must have raised at least a few questions in her mind.

Through the years, Leonard tried his hand at a variety of odd jobs, including water heater installation. Sadly, the man had an uncanny knack for getting fired, usually blaming his predicament on anyone but himself. His social interactions became nonexistent.

One of the few memories I retain of my grandfather is of him standing on the back porch of their little house in Berrien Springs. He is smoking a cigarette, possibly a Winston, if memory of its red-and-white packaging serves me correctly. As the picture forms yet again in my mind's eye, I wonder if the habit provided the only relief he knew for a mind fraught with anxiety and a thousand regrets of what might have been. After all, as one expert explains, due to the chemical effects of nicotine on the brain, "People with serious mental illness often are heavy smokers. . . . This potentially positive aspect of smoking may explain why, in 1948, *the Journal of the American Medical Association* stated that 'from a psychological point of view, in all probability more can be said in behalf of smoking as a form of escape from tension than against it.'"[2]

This all leads me to ask a painfully pointed question surrounding my own psyche: Would I have acted any differently had I been born in 1885 as Leonard was? To me, this question is not far afield from the arrogant belief that I would not have called for Jesus' crucifixion had I been part of the maniacal crowd gathered that world-changing weekend in Jerusalem so long ago.

I am filled with humility and gratefulness that I was born in an era different from that of my grandfather. True,

not every corporate pharmaceutical adventure has resulted in a perfect fix, but scientific and therapeutic commu-
nities have worked wonders in my behalf. As a result,
I am hopeful that my sons will not find it necessary to
spring me from a padded cell.

Leonard Fishell died of a heart attack at age 68. I don't
know if he had a bona fide anxiety disorder, but accompanying him into the cold earth were some pretty odd
behaviors, left to play out in at least a few descendants.

So is all my trouble to be laid at the base of a sys-
temically diseased family tree? A closer look at a couple
of other revealing branches is forthcoming. (Hey, don't
gloat. Like it or not, some pretty colorful characters play
a big role in your present behavior too!) In my case, it all
adds up to a challenging and sometimes downright uncomfortable inheritance, a mysterious ball of intra-psychic yarn that I continue striving to unravel.

Happily, I did eventually finish reading *Nyla and the
White Crocodile*. But the experience was merely a pre-
cursor to a growing range of troubling symptoms that in-
terfered with my daily life.

By fifth grade I was an increasingly anxious person. All
was not well at home, and my anxieties were intensified
by the uncertainty of my proper place in a new school.
Obsessive thoughts came and went, usually driven by my
continuing desire to always "do the right thing."

Situated close to Lake Michigan, during the winter
months our community often found itself buried under a
thick blanket of lake-effect snow. During this same time
of year, January 1-April 15 to be exact, my accountant
father, on the other hand, was buried under a thick blan-

ket of tax returns. His daily work routine during those months went like this:

8:00 A.M.—office
12:15 P.M.—home for lunch
12:35 P.M.—nap
1:00 P.M.—office
5:30 P.M.—home for supper
6:15 P.M.—nap
7:00 P.M.—office
9:45 P.M.—home for sleep

Our family faithfully observed a biblical Sabbath from Friday evening sunset to Saturday evening sunset. Sometimes Dad had to do tax work on Saturday nights, though, and every Sunday afternoon found him either at home or back at the office, magically punching adding machine buttons without looking at them. (To this day I contend that Ripley's Believe It or Not! missed out on a good item for their Sunday column when they failed to feature my father's astonishing tax season dexterity.)

One bitterly cold evening I'd headed off to my bedroom to say my bedside prayers. But that night the demons of obsession were once again on the loose.

". . . and please bless the missionaries in China, and help my brother to do well in history class, and . . ." My prayer continued until my eyelids began sliding south. But I wasn't finished, not by a long shot.

". . . and be with my teacher, and the people who are fighting in Viet Nam, and . . ." On and on my prayer continued; it had to, because many needs of which I'd become aware had yet to be presented for heavenly processing.

Or did I really have to pray about *everything*? My father might be able to answer that question, I reasoned. Perhaps it was providential that this particular night found him working on tax returns at the dining room table. Still, should I distract him from his laser-like focus on credit and debit columns? But if I didn't, sleep might not arrive until sunrise. This hyper-conscientious kid needed to know just how deep and wide my prayers needed to be, so I figured I had to take the risk. I trundled down the staircase and into the dining room.

"Um, I was wondering about something," I said softly.

Dad's fingers paused above the adding machine keys and he looked up at me. "About what?" he asked.

"Well, um, how do I know who I should be praying for? It's taking a long time."

Dad's ability to disguise his befuddlement should've earned him an Oscar. I suppose by then he'd seen enough of my behavior to be prepared for most anything.

"Well, I think if you just pray about the most important things, and maybe your family, that should be fine," he responded.

I nodded, then headed back upstairs to my bedroom. Arriving at my bedside, I once again knelt and resumed my intercession.

". . . and help Aunt Edith and Uncle Everett to be safe tomorrow, and be with that person our teacher said has that bad sickness, whatever it was . . ."

It took just a few minutes for the realization to set in: my well-intentioned father's counsel was having zero effect. Somewhere in the back of my mind I feared that

God would cut me out of the final heavenly action if I messed up on this prayer thing. After all, didn't He expect me to be perfect like Him?

I made a second trek downstairs. This time I stood in silence, waiting for my father to complete his current calculation. At last he looked up at me.

"I guess I don't get it," I said, my voice now tinged with growing distress. "I mean, will something bad happen to someone if I don't pray for them?"

I could tell the barrel holding my father's reserve of patience was beginning to drain at a quickened rate. Still, he did his best. "No, you don't have to pray about *everything*. That would be impossible. God knows what's in your heart. Just cover the basics and let it go at that." He returned to the business at hand.

Simple enough, and pragmatic to boot. This should be a piece of cake.

And for millions of kids saying their prayers that night, it probably was. But not for me.

"... and thank you that our furnace is working, and be with Mr. Evert as he drives his heating oil delivery truck, and help his sons to do good in school ..."

A few more utterances and, just like the night I'd struggled to read *Nyla and the White Crocodile*, I was exhausted and fighting tears.

My third trip downstairs was not well-received. "Just say 'Amen' and go to sleep!" my exasperated father instructed.

Wearily, I climbed the stairs for the last time that night. Sleep eventually washed over me. A boy can stay awake praying for only so long.

Society's interest in spirituality waxes and wanes. What

does not change is the fact that most people have spiritual beliefs of one kind or another. It's important to address those beliefs in the quest for mental health.

Consider one study of people battling depression, which often accompanies anxiety disorders. The researchers "sought to assess spirituality in depressed patients and evaluate whether the degree of initial depressive symptoms and response to pharmacotherapy treatment has a correlation with degree of spirituality and belief in God."[3] What conclusions were drawn? "The findings suggest that greater spirituality is associated with less severe depression. Moreover, the degree to which the measures of depressive symptom severity, hopelessness, and cognitive distortions improved over the course of eight weeks was significantly greater for those patients who were more spiritual."[4]

Whether depression, anxiety, or another mental health challenge, the role of spirituality in the recovery process should not be underestimated. Appendix C provides tips to help you nurture your spiritual self in appropriate and healing ways. Making an effort in this can have a very real and positive effect in your pursuit of rising above anxiety disorders.*

*Chapter 4 looks at an especially problematic brand of spirituality known as "perfectionism."

THREE

STEPS IN THE WRONG DIRECTION

Mental disorders pay no mind to class distinction. For example, the list of well-known individuals battling OCD includes:

▶ Cameron Diaz, actress and former fashion model. Diaz has publicly admitted she habitually rubs doorknobs so hard before opening doors to clean them that the original paint on the doorknobs fades afterward. She also washes her hands "many times" each day.[1]

▶ Howie Mandel, Canadian comedian and actor. Mandel can't shake hands with anyone due to *mysophobia*, a fear of dirt and germs. For this reason Howie shaves his head—it helps him feel cleaner.[2]

▶ David Beckham, former professional soccer player. He's obsessed with order and is always putting things into pairs, in hotels, his closet and the refrigerator.[3]

▶ Jane Horrocks, English stage, screen and television

actress, voice artist, musician, and singer. She used to count her blinks.[4]

There are many others, but this list provides encouragement that suffering from obsessive-compulsive disorder does not automatically mean setting one's dreams aside. Who knows what game-changers throughout the annals of history spent their lives repeating prayers and counting things?

The popular picture of the "typical" OCD sufferer is someone who washes his or her hands throughout the day, then checks multiple times that night to be sure the doors are locked. As the website Disabled World states, "[Obsessive-compulsive disorder] is most commonly characterized by a subject's obsessive drive to perform a particular task or set of tasks, compulsions commonly termed rituals."[5] This type of behavior was on full display in the TV series *Monk*. "After the unsolved murder of his wife, Adrian Monk develops obsessive-compulsive disorder, which includes his terror of germs and contamination. His condition costs him his job as a prominent homicide detective in the San Francisco Police Department, but he continues to solve crimes with the help of his assistant and his former boss."[6]

The preceding description of OCD may be true in a certain perfunctory clinical sense, but the disorder and its extended family members spans a much wider gamut than such a definition implies. The vocational, relational, and emotional fallout can be debilitating.

So just how many people suffer from obsessive-compulsive disorder? According to Dr. H. Blair Simpson, Professor of Clinical Psychiatry, Columbia University, and Director of the Anxiety Disorders Clinic and the

Center for OCD and Related Disorders at New York State Psychiatric Institute in New York City, "[OCD] is relatively much more common than people thought; it is about two percent lifetime prevalence and in comparison, schizophrenia is one percent."[7] In other words, in the United States alone, at any given time over six million people are dealing with some form of obsessive-compulsive disorder.

Regarding onset and symptoms, Dr. Simpson states, "About half of the cases of OCD will start by age 19 and in comparison, about half of the cases of depression start at age 32. Typically, the course of it once you get it is typically chronic, waxing and waning symptoms. . . . The severity of it is much more than . . . other anxiety disorders. If you have the disorder, the vast majority will have moderate or severe symptoms. If you add that all up—early onset, how common it is, chronic course, and severe symptoms—you can see that it can be very disabling. What happens is that people get the disorder relatively early in life and it can get them off track."[8]

No kidding.

Again, technically speaking, obsessive-compulsive disorder is no longer classified as an anxiety disorder. In his book, *The Man Who Couldn't Stop*, writer and editor David Adam points out that "In May, 2013, the American Psychiatric Association (APA) officially reclassified OCD as a different type of mental illness. It's now one of the obsessive-compulsive and related disorders, a new group of . . . OCD spectrum disorders [including] body dysmorphic disorder, hair-pulling, skin-picking and hoarding disorder."[9]

Unfortunately, the reclassification doesn't make OCD any easier to deal with.

To this day, the smell of chlorine makes me want to run in the opposite direction. Not because years ago I unwittingly mixed ammonia with Clorox and nearly killed myself with its deadly fumes. No, its pungent aroma carries me even further back in my personal history, to the YMCA in Niles, Michigan.

I don't remember how old I was, perhaps 10. Whatever my age, Mom had decided that my brother Dave and I needed to learn how to swim properly. Since the closest facility offering swimming classes was in Niles, about ten miles from our house, the die was cast.

My brother Dave seemed OK with diving right into the lessons, but I was a basket case. In fact, I expressed such anguish that, after entering the building with my swim trunks and towel in hand, Mom finally caved to my whining. While she stayed inside the building to watch my brother's progress, I headed back out to the car and curled up in the back seat. A few minutes later, the YMCA manager stuck his head through the open car window.

"Hey, bud," the man greeted a little awkwardly. "Your mother asked me to come out here and talk to you."

Great.

"So, what seems to be the problem?" he asked.

I shrugged. "I guess I'm just kinda scared," I finally said, my voice barely above a whisper.

"About what?"

I paused, then said, "I don't know. I'm just scared."

At this juncture, the well-intentioned facility manager reached deep into his storehouse of reassurances, including the fact that the swimming instructors also happened to be formally trained in lifesaving techniques. This all made little impact on me. The gentleman headed back inside. He'd done his best, but I'm not sure he'd been trained to bolster the courage of someone afflicted with such insecurities.

Though I did eventually take swimming lessons elsewhere, the YMCA episode made a lasting impact on me. What was I *really* scared of? I realize that dipping one's toes for the first time into an Olympic-size swimming pool is a common childhood fear. And of course there's the dreaded "deep end." Who in their right mind would risk so much simply to allow someone to check a box indicating that their little charge had touched the bottom and lived to tell about it?

Still, there's something about the incident that dredges up the idea that it somehow exceeded normal childhood fear. Could it be that my deeper fear lay in the fact that Mom would be perched high in the observation balcony, with no immediate access to her son should the worst occur?

I don't want to make too much of this memory, because most kids go through a stage of separation anxiety. But most of them get over it.

I have no way of knowing if this particular episode foreshadowed future adult separation anxieties. I do know that the sense of shame I felt as I walked back to the car that day would surface again and again in later years as I struggled to rise above my anxiety disorders.

Toward the beginning of sixth grade, my teacher, Mrs. Oster, asked me a question that should have surprised me. "I've noticed that you do very well with arithmetic. Would you be willing to help tutor some of the others who are having trouble in this area?"

This is nothing short of amusing, as these days I consider myself "challenged" in anything related to numbers. But when Mrs. Oster asked me that question, I quickly said yes. At the time, I knew beyond the shadow of a doubt that I was really good at arithmetic. Soon I reveled in the deep satisfaction that accompanied my new role as a sixth-grade peer tutor.

But by seventh grade, I was on a downhill slide. I started seventh grade in the remedial math class. So what happened between grades six and seven?

First of all, only later did I realize that academic placement testing had resulted in my being sentenced to the "second tier" sixth-grade classroom. In other words, I had failed to make the cut to be placed in the classroom into which the supposedly "brightest" students called home. But the dullest pencil in the box I was not, so I quickly rose to the top of my lesser intellectually gifted class.

The arithmetic column on my sixth-grade report card provides graphic evidence that my fame as a child prodigy was fleeting. It still resides in a dust-covered box in my attic. Over the course of six grading periods it reads precisely as follows: A, A-, B, B-, C, C-.

TGSV: thank God for summer vacation.

Nobody, including myself, could figure out what was happening. Today I have at least a few clues. A popular 1960s TV series provides an instructive metaphor.

Get Smart featured the bumbling efforts of Agent 86, played by funnyman Don Adams. Fortunately, sidekick Barbara Feldon, Agent 99, usually saved the day for her beloved fellow agent. Adams and Feldon were employed by CONTROL, a secret government counter-intelligence agency. The nemesis organization against which they fought so valiantly—and hilariously—was known as KAOS.

Control and chaos (properly spelled) are pertinent descriptors for the two sides engaged in a battle raging within my adolescent mind. None of this was at a conscious level. An evidence of its reality, however, was my increasing inability to remain focused on the task at hand, including addition, subtraction, and common denominators. Instead of growing my math skills, more and more of my mental energy was devoted toward controlling . . . something . . . so as not to be overwhelmed by emotional chaos. As long as I could distract myself from any kind of mental or emotional anguish, things were OK. At least, that's the message my subconscious mind relayed on a regular basis to my behavioral control center. So I embarked upon a nonstop campaign of misdeeds and tomfoolery to keep my mind preoccupied. These mischievous forays included passing secret messages to my best friend by stuffing them into a shotgun shell and hurling the projectile across the classroom, to plotting and executing a subversive out-the-window escape during art class. Admittedly, I liked the attention my miscreant attitude brought my direction, even though I knew punishment awaited. I admit that my regrettable behavior was likely not totally the result of psychological distress. But something beyond typical adolescent misbehavior was going on. Was I a bored, creative kid trying to maintain sanity within a too-structured environment? Probably. Were brain chemicals changing and rearranging to meet the forthcoming normal challenges of youth and young adulthood? Of course. But I'm pretty sure these adventures in delinquency also represented an effort to both distract from and control the chaos building within my psyche.

Just as with the YMCA episode, I don't want to make too much of this after-the-fact self-analysis. Still, later therapy did seem to affirm my conclusions on the subject. One clinical psychologist likened my activity to a NASA mission control center, with me in the controller's chair, determined that nothing would go wrong. But in my case, it did.

In the Bible, Jesus urges humans to not fret about anything. Matthew 6:25 records this specific command: "Do not worry about your life, what you will eat or drink; or about your body" (New International Version).[10] If my hopes for an eventual heavenly mansion depended on that last part, I was in real trouble. Not only did worry come naturally to me as an adolescent, but my body was usually the focal point of my uncertainties. Talk about double spiritual trouble! Somatic alarms sounded on an almost daily basis. Many of these disquieting concerns were appropriate; after all, my body *was* changing. But other disturbing thought patterns simply blindsided me, with no apparent connection to reality. One particularly intense episode was triggered by the death of a Detroit Lions' football player.

Chuck Hughes was an astonishingly talented high school and college athlete, and several football records for the University of Texas at El Paso still bear his name.

By 1971, Chuck Hughes was making his mark as a wide receiver and special teams player for the Lions. On October 24 of that year, playing in Detroit against the Chicago Bears, Chuck ran a pass route on a play that he was not part of (the pass was intended for tight end Charlie Sanders). Jogging back to the huddle, Hughes collapsed on the Bears' fifteen-yard line. Some players thought it was a fake injury and that he was trying to buy the Lions some extra time. But when Bears' linebacker Dick Butkus began frantically signaling for help, everyone in the stadium knew something bad had happened.

Chuck's teammates were informed of his death before they left the stadium that day. The autopsy revealed that, as a result of advanced arteriosclerosis, his coronary arteries were 75 percent blocked. During the game, a blood clot had completely cut off the circulation to his heart.[11]

In Michigan where I lived, Hughes' death was a big sports story. I didn't like tuning in to such realities, however, and that's probably why I got the facts a little twisted up along the way. The blood clot in the heart somehow became a brain tumor in my version of the tale, and I had the unrelenting conviction (OK, an obsession) that I just might be next. *What was that twitch I just felt up there? Was something about to burst inside my brain? How can I stop thinking about a possible brain tumor ... brain tumor ... brain tumor?*

My parents knew something was wrong with their youngest son, but I felt too embarrassed to come out and give them a full accounting of my current cognitive trials. Still, they must have felt an obligation to do something, because soon enough I ended up in the doctor's office. There, I told the physician that I was worried that I might have a brain tumor. He pushed here and there on my head and asked if anything hurt. When I told him it didn't, he quickly concluded that neurosurgery would not be necessary. Oh, the issue was definitely all in my head, just not in the way I'd been envisioning. It's actually called hypochondriasis, or health anxiety, and it is very prevalent among people who have anxiety. Some experts believe that hypochondriasis is a form of obsessive-compulsive disorder. In this case, it's an obsession with health. There may also be an underlying fear of dying. The brain tumor obsession continued for a few months. As that crisis faded over time, others took its place. The god Pan still waited patiently in hiding, planning a future all-out surprise attack. In the meantime, there was plenty else to occupy my anxious mind.

Shop. Industrial Arts. Tech Ed. The names changed over time, but the basic goal of such classes remained the same: showing adolescent (mainly) males how to build a bookcase and change a lawnmower spark plug without severing a limb or doing other bodily damage.

Our seventh-grade shop class was held in a building far away from the main school facility. A couple of times each week, we'd get out of geography class and we guys would walk a quarter mile or so to the shop building. (The girls took Home Economics during the same period.) Upon our arrival, we were greeted by our instructor, Mr. Swenson. The pleasant, shop apron-wearing Swede did his best to maintain the interest of his largely disinterested group of students. The man was actually rather brilliant. Besides possessing vast knowledge about various trades, he had earned both amateur radio and private pilot licenses. He should have earned a medal for having to teach the likes of us how to saw a board in half.

One day after shop class I experienced a weird phenomenon. That memorable autumn day as I strolled along on my way back to the main school building, I began taking unusual notice of my steps. My buddy Tom was chattering away about his latest girlfriend, which usually held at least marginal interest. But not that day; I was too busy studying my feet—and mentally counted each step they took. *Twenty-two . . . twenty-three . . . .* This wouldn't have been such a big deal, except I couldn't seem to *stop* counting them. *Sixty-eight . . . sixty-nine . . .*

I counted my steps all the way back to school. For the rest of the day, little surges of panic came and went. Why had it suddenly become necessary to count my steps, and why hadn't I been able to stop?

Over the next few weeks, walking became a draining chore, not physically, but mentally and emotionally. My anxiety increased as I realized that the only cure for this weird behavior would be to stop walking. This is not written as hyperbole; it was reality as I experienced it, as obsessive-compulsive behavior took deeper root.

A look at tinnitus may prove helpful. Tinnitus is a constant ringing or buzzing in the ears, a condition that most experts agree presently has no cure. (I have tinnitus big-time, as do many anxiety-prone individuals.) The main affordable "treatment" for tinnitus is to increase the sound of something else until the sufferer can no longer hear the ringing or buzzing sound. More expensive therapies help to train the brain to ignore the unremitting ear sounds, but the sounds themselves are still present. Whatever the chosen remedy, the current proven therapies for tinnitus basically revolve around some form of distraction rather than resulting in an actual cure.

While there are tales of tinnitus suffers committing suicide as a result of having no way to stop the bothersome sounds, I will simply say that it seems plausible. After all, to these sufferers, there appears to be no solution, reasonable or otherwise. They literally feel doomed to a life of enduring sounds in their head that go away only in their sleep. They can't reach inside their ear canal and turn off the whistling or buzzing sounds. With prospects for resolution so dim, who wouldn't be ready to take desperate measures?

I do not mean to sound melodramatic, but maladies such as tinnitus can reveal the depth of despair to which a seemingly little annoyance can lead someone. Counting steps doesn't seem like such a big deal—until you realize that you may never be able to stop doing it.

For a White dude, I've always had pretty good rhythm. Maybe that's because I've had so much practice.

About the same time that I started counting my steps, another behavior manifested itself, which stays with me to this day: clicking my teeth while counting in rhythm. Just as I don't *want* to count my steps, I don't *want* to click my teeth and count. Also similarly, this rhythmic spinoff has nothing to do with enumerating objects. I don't drive down a country road, spot the usual suspects, and begin counting the pasture's occupants. *One cow, two cows, three cows.* Rather, I simply "say" certain numbers in my head while clicking my teeth. Number *sequences*, such as 17, 18, 19 or 37, 38, 39 frequently tap dance their way onto my mental stage.

So what exactly prompts this particular compulsive thought process? In my case, I think it may function as some kind of "filler material"—a subliminal control mechanism. Leave too much blank space between thoughts, and something really bad might happen. Better to fill that space with counting and teeth clicking than accidentally to allow a mental catastrophe to strike! By now, of course, the whole thing is so deeply ingrained that perhaps it has become more habit than a behavior, producing a bona fide stream-of-consciousness benefit.

As I have repeatedly mentioned (a little OCD humor there), I do not *want* to count in my head. I am not wired like *Sesame Street's* Count, for whom numbers provide a high similar to that of an illegal narcotic. No, for me counting is a wearisome mental function that I have no natural ability to resist.

Although counting and clicking can happen anytime, anywhere, sometimes it takes a musical twist, with the numbers replaced by musical lyrics. For example, a while back as I hiked a portion of the Appalachian Trail, I found myself clicking my teeth to the tune of Peter, Paul, and Mary's "Puff the Magic Dragon." Who knows? Maybe modern sound technology will soon allow my mental music to be digitized and made available as a download. Weirder behaviors have made people rich and famous. But until I can take my cognitive pastime to the bank, it's not much fun.

FOUR

HEAVENLY DYSFUNCTION

"Now, here's the play." Grant was the quarterback for our ninth-grade intramural football squad, and he was about to pull a surprise play on the opposing team. "Randy, I'm going to hand off the ball to you. Just head for the goal line, and we'll block for you."

Far beyond a surprise play, this was more like a "they've got-to-be-kidding" kind of gridiron strategy. The quarterback was going to hand off the football to *me?* This was the first official athletic game I'd ever played in! I was abysmal at sports. I'd once been pitted against the slowest runner in PE class, who ended up beating me! First, I'd earned the title of slowest runner, and now this? Actually, having the football in my hands was surely destined to prove just what a sorry excuse for a player I really was.

But before I could publicly question my quarterback's play call, he broke the huddle, and I lined up behind him. "Forty-two! Six! Six! Hike!" I watched as Grant's right arm swung out with the football. Sure enough, as I ran up beside him, he stuffed it into my belly and shouted, "Run for the goal line!" Apparently, the surprise play was working, because what to my wondering eyes should appear but an opening! I ran with all my might toward the general area where the goal line resided (I didn't know which stripe it actually was).

"That's enough, Randy, you can stop running!" Grant finally shouted. "You scored."

My football career was off to a winning start! As it turned out, that touchdown would be the one and only of my entire high school career. A week later, an unrelenting weariness overcame me, and I was diagnosed with hepatitis A—a viral infection of the liver. Pinpointing its cause can be pretty tough, and in my case, just how I contracted hepatitis remains a mystery. The doctor made clear that I was to stay physically inactive for the duration of my illness, and to keep taking it easy for several weeks afterward.

Goodbye football, hello bed rest.

Hepatitis A isn't the worst form of the virus. Still, its effects lingered for many weeks. Eventually, I was able to return to my after-school job of potting plants at a local nursery. It was more like a groundcover assembly line, really: fill pot with soil using left hand, stuff rooted cutting into pot with right hand, place in tray, repeat. It was a perfect job for an obsessive-compulsive personality, although I don't remember if I counted every plant I potted. The intensity of my OCD symptoms varied, depending on what else was consuming my mental energy at the time. I've often wondered, though, about any possible link between physical and mental illness. Does one contribute toward the other in any way whatsoever? According to MentalHealthcare.gov: "Many factors contribute to mental health problems, including biological factors, such as genes, *physical illness,* injury, or brain chemistry [italics mine]."[1] Perhaps future research will reveal to what extent this is true.

Currently, the weight of evidence does not seem to suggest that physical illness is a primary trigger of anxiety disorders. Still, research does indicate that there can be a correlation between physical illness and anxiety disorders *in some cases.* A summary of one such study states: "The mechanisms of association between anxiety disorders and physical conditions remain unknown, although several possibilities should be considered." For example, the presence of an illness may cause worry and anxiety that eventually becomes serious enough to qualify as an anxiety disorder, the presence of an anxiety disorder could trigger biological processes that contribute to illness or a third condition, such as a substance abuse disorder, could be linked to both."[2]

By this time, trying to control my mental environment through distraction masquerading as misbehavior had found a comfortable place in my arsenal of coping mechanisms. But there were always boundaries I refused to cross. In a twisted sort of way, I believe some of my dysfunctional thought patterns proved to be my salvation from some truly destructive behaviors. "You'd make a very good alcoholic," a psychologist once told me. He meant that plenty of people in my situation choose self-medication with alcohol or illegal drugs to squelch their anxiety.

Self-medication through alcohol or any other substance is risky business. Elizabeth Vargas of ABC's *20/20* wishes she could have a do-over. "I regret that I self-medicated my anxiety," she said in an interview for *AARP Bulletin*. "I started drinking in my 20s. I was drinking to unwind and to not feel so anxious. I told nobody, even though I had a panic attack on live television in Chicago. I was afraid they would say, 'If you have anxiety, you don't belong on national television.'"[3]

Vargas tells how a well-intentioned but apparently ill-informed medical professional helped to push her down the wrong path: "After the birth of my second child, something was wrong—very, very wrong. I was convinced I had postpartum depression. [My doctor] sent me to an expert who said, 'No, you're just anxious—go home and have a glass of wine.' So I went home and had several glasses of wine. I fell off a cliff."[4]

I never met Floyd Bolenbaugh, but I'm told he was quite a character. The last name alone makes most people think of spares and strikes. But whenever I mention the name and folks begin to snicker, I get a tad defensive. After all, the man *was* my grandfather.

According to the 1940 Michigan census, Floyd was born in Ohio in 1897. His occupation is listed as "laborer." My mother describes him in even less dignified terms. Floyd made his exit from the family when Mom was just 10, but apparently, he made enough of an impression that she does not harbor particularly warm memories. In fact, she seldom speaks of her real father, but I do remember her mentioning the man's affection for hard liquor.

I'm cautious in asking my mother for details about her father; the last thing I want to do is dredge up painful memories at this stage of her life (she is 89 as I write). As a result, just how the man's gene pool impacts mine will likely remain at least a partial mystery. Was Floyd

Bolenbaugh an anxious person? Did he have a tendency to count things and click his teeth? Did he get panicky riding a horse or driving a Studebaker alone at night?

When I recall the therapist's comment about my potential for becoming a good alcoholic, I think about Floyd. Maybe he was doing the best he could to deal with circumstances—or a mind—that somehow seemed just a little beyond his control. Perhaps someday I'll have the chance to ask him. When it comes to passing the heavenly entry test, I'm told God takes a lot more into consideration than good behavior.

Self-medication should be a non-starter for anyone battling anxiety. If you've already headed down that path, consider it yet another reason to seek qualified professional help.

In my case, I was simply afraid of what those kinds of substances might do to me. Would sloe gin cause me to lose control? What kind of chaos might result from indulging in marijuana? No, I couldn't risk falling over the phobic edge into an indefinable and possibly irreversible mental morass. Besides, it would make God mad, wouldn't it? Bad theology, but it's funny how even a twisted rationale can work to a person's advantage.

"Psychiatry has a long tradition of dismissing and attacking religious experience." That's what Simon Dein, FRCPsych, PhD, wrote in an informative article in *Psychiatric Times*.[5] Dein goes on to say that "Religion has often been seen by mental health professionals in Western societies as irrational, outdated, and dependency forming and has been viewed to result in emotional instability."[6] Additionally, "Albert Ellis, the founder of rational emotive therapy, wrote in the *Journal of Consulting and Clinical Psychology* that there was an irrefutable causal relationship between religion and emotional and mental illness."[7]

If the latter thesis is correct, I should resign myself to a terminal state of hopelessness. However, those statements were made years ago and do not reflect later research that puts a more positive spin on the subject. At present, according to Dein, "The evidence suggests that, on balance, religious involvement is generally conducive to *better* mental health [italics mine]."[8]

Hallelujah! Looks like my core belief system may not be leading me toward the insane asylum after all. Still, there can be little doubt that certain brands of religious experience lend themselves to emotional and mental dysfunction. My own spiritual heritage has on occasion provided ample doses of spiritual radioactivity for its more susceptible adherents. In bygone years, the main message that many of us received—intentional or otherwise—was the need to become perfect, lest God bar the heavenly gates to our entrance. Behavior modification was central, with rules and lists of acceptable and unacceptable activities receiving a great deal of attention. In the matter of Christianity, the gospel—the "good news" that Jesus' life, death, and resurrection accomplished for us what we could never do for ourselves—got little play in the doctrinal shuffle. Too often the Bible's call to moral goodness (or "relative perfection," in theological terms) became confused with "perfectionism," a joy-crushing, unattainable goal that is considered an emotional disorder in mental health terms. This type of thinking,

[56]

which also involves what some call "legalism," is not unique to my denomination. Legalism can play an unhelpful role in mental health issues for many people, regardless of religious affiliation. It's still a problem in some Christian denominations.

The trouble sets in when our field of vision becomes so narrow that we can see only small strokes on a much larger canvas. Instead of daily seeking to love God, our neighbors, and ourselves with gentleness and compassion, we try harder and harder to please the authority figures whose moral voices we've come to internalize. Paying heed to certain of those voices is healthy—physically, spiritually, and sociologically. But as any cult member rescued from bondage will testify, it pays to do a serious background check on leaders before checking into the commune.

Jonestown, Heaven's Gate, and Westboro Baptist Church aside, even those of us not taken with such outfits can fall victim to our own supersensitive conscience. We take our religious experience seriously and work hard at living up to our understanding of its tenets. Unfortunately, too often our pursuit of becoming a better person quickly escalates into an anxiety- and guilt-ridden trek to Never Good Enough land. It doesn't take long for us to throw up our hands in frustration, realizing that we'll never live up to others' or our own self-imposed standards. We develop a laser-like focus on what it takes to be good rather than celebrating an experience rooted in spiritual *freedom*. Uncertain of where we really stand with God, peace escapes us and is soon replaced by unremitting spiritual anxiety.

Biblical Christianity, or course, harbors a powerful antidote to this dark scenario: grace. But sometimes even this healing balm comes hard for those driven by a deep-ly-embedded fear of displeasing the Divine—or some other spiritual authority figure.

Depending on where any organization—religious or otherwise—finds itself on its developmental journey, certain core propositions are likely to receive more attention than others. Often this is a good thing, but at other times, unless helpful course corrections occur, decision-making and organizational development continue to revolve around the same limited set of propositions. Nobody stops to look at the big picture and allow it to be revealed in its proper time and place. For example, in the Christian tradition, protocol, counsel, and other directives may be taken out of context and misapplied, ultimately receiving more emphasis than the Bible itself. In the end, a healthier and more spiritually appropriate picture fails to emerge.

Adherents to any belief system, from Atheists to Lutherans to Zoroastrianists, harbor what they consider "special truths" as part of their unique message and sub-culture. Healthy, dynamic spiritual enterprises nurture the mature use of precious spiritual resources—written, spoken, and otherwise. Not doing so can result in an anx-iety-laden spiritual dysfunction, the effects of which are not easily undone.

Whenever I learn of someone abandoning a certain tenet of their faith, I wonder how much of their decision was based on carrying a burden they were never asked to bear.

Karl Marx said, "Religion is the sigh of the oppressed creature, the heart of a heartless world, and the soul of soulless conditions. It is the opium of the people." I hate to give Marx credit for anything, but he may have been at least partially right on this one. On the one hand, religious movements have spawned some of the greatest positive changes in history. But whenever religious thought and dogma becomes an end unto itself, it can lead to deadly consequences, leaving a regrettable impact on the geo-political landscape, as well as on an individual's heart, soul, and mind.

The late Anglican canon J. B. Phillips addresses the distorted idea some people have of trying to please God. In his classic book *Your God Is Too Small*, Phillips writes;

> "Of all the false gods there is probably no greater nuisance in the spiritual world than the 'god of one hundred percent.' For he is plausible. It can so easily be argued that since God is Perfection, and since He asks the complete loyalty of His creatures, then the best way of serving, pleasing, and worshipping Him is to set up absolute one-hundred-percent standards and see to it that we obey them. After all, did not Christ say, Be ye perfect'?

> "This one-hundred-percent standard is a real menace to Christians of various schools of thought, and has led quite a number of sensitive conscientious people to what is popularly called a 'nervous breakdown.' And it has taken the joy and spontaneity out of the Christian lives of many more who dimly realize that what was meant to be a life of 'perfect freedom' has become an anxious slavery.

> "It is probably only people of certain backgrounds

and temperaments who will find the 'one-hundred-percent god' a terrible tyrant. A young athletic extrovert may talk glibly enough of being 'one-hundred-percent pure, honest, loving and unselfish.' . . . He is not the type to analyse his own motives. . . .

"But the conscientious, sensitive, imaginative person who is somewhat lacking in self-confidence and inclined to introspection, will find one-hundred-percent perfection truly terrifying. The more he thinks of God's demand the more guilty and miserable he will become, and he cannot see any way out of his impasse. If he reduces the one-hundred-percent he is betraying his own spiritual vision, and the very God who might have helped him is the Author (or so he imagines) of the terrific demands! No wonder he often 'breaks down.'"[9]

The relationship between spirituality and anxiety is complex. Is there really a cause-and-effect dynamic at work between religion and certain aspects of mental dysfunction, or is this just one theologian's take on the matter?

In his book *The Man Who Couldn't Stop*, author Dan Adam provides some intriguing insight surrounding religion and obsessive-compulsive disorder:

"Psychologists who have studied this link between OCD and religion say it could come down to ways of thinking called dysfunctional beliefs. Most people have dysfunctional beliefs, which we usually pick up in childhood. They are not mental disorders, they are lenses placed across our cognition. They distort the way we perceive the world and can help explain why different people interpret identical situations in different ways."[10]

Adam, who suffers from OCD, goes on to explain that dysfunctional beliefs often result in what is called "thought-action fusion." This is a technical way of saying that obsessive people begin to place undue emphasis on thoughts and even begin fearing that they might somehow unwillingly act upon those thoughts. This can have a strong impact on conscientious, spiritually minded individuals:

"Psychologists say that thought-action fusion could explain the way OCD shows itself among religious people. Some Christians, for instance, are often distressed to discover they can even conceive of sin. Their impure thoughts, they believe, must show they are not as devout as they hoped. Thought-action fusion makes these people believe that their thoughts—their thoughts alone—represent moral failure that makes them more likely to face God's judgment. These distressing sinful thoughts are of course ego-dystonic, they run contrary to the individual's faith. This makes the person more likely to try to suppress the thoughts, and so for the thoughts to return."[11]

Interestingly, studies show that thought-action fusion crosses all religious lines. So—does religion cause OCD?

Probably not. Again, Adam sheds light on the issue:

"One reason we can be confident that religion does not cause OCD is that obsessions and compulsions crop up with similar frequency in both secular and strictly religious countries. But, although the total number of people with OCD is unaffected by a country's religious leanings, the more religious a place, the more the clinical obsessions of these people centre on religious issues. *Religion might not provoke obsessions, but it does provide an outlet for them.*"[12]

Whenever I hear the term *perfect storm*, I think, *Exactly whom is it that considers this storm "perfect"?* I suppose meteorologists appreciate a stupendous mix of nature's forces, but most people who face such a whopper-type weather event are nervously hunkered down, hoping it will soon pass.

I'm pretty sure my situation was the result of a "perfect" storm of "nature and nurture;" that is, a combination of biology and the way I grew up. This is hardly a breakthrough scientific announcement. After all, who *isn't* deeply affected by those two things? It's just that, from what I can tell, some just get a little more of this and a little less of that. I am offended by the idea that "God made you just the way you are." If He did, I don't have much confidence in His compassion or creative capabilities. Yes, I believe God's hand is mysteriously involved in all creation. But I've found great logic in the tenet that humanity is caught in an unseen battle between good and evil—there's simply too much evidence to suggest otherwise. We are collateral damage of this battle—physically, mentally, morally, and spiritually. One reason I continue to believe in God is that I want someday to see who He intended each of us to be, minus the complications.

If I had to blame one or the other, given what I know now, I'd say that a lot more nature (biology) goes into anxiety disorders than nurture (environment). Too bad I didn't come to that conclusion much sooner. I might have altogether avoided what I call the "lost decades"—those years spent trying so desperately to convince myself that I could fix the problem by simply thinking the right thoughts and employing the latest behavior modification techniques. It's true that psychotherapy can be immensely helpful. After all, we still must challenge those beliefs that keep us from leaning into the winds of our anxieties. But for now, as I battled an increasing bevy of challenges, things would grow much worse before they got better. The perfect storm still raged.

FIVE

NEW PLACES, NEW FACES

"He ain't nothin'." Such was the lanky jock's appraisal of my basketball skills at the new school I'd just begun attending.

I was on a quest to spice up my teenage life, and my parents had agreed to allow me to attend an out-of-state religious boarding high school. A trip to Mardi Gras it was not, but given my background, I was stepping outside my comfort zone by a substantial margin.

Some 250 miles from my hometown in Michigan, Wisconsin Academy was part of our denomination's vast parochial education system. It was the middle of my junior year, and I hoped to reset my life. Planting myself in a new school setting where no one knew me would be fertile ground for creating a totally new persona. Two and half years into high school had done nothing to move me off the bottom rung of the social ladder. The time had come to move up.

But things were not off to a healthy start. It was my first night at the school (I started mid-school year), and all the students who wished to participate had gathered for a regular weeknight "recreational time" in the school's gymnasium. I tagged along, determined to take some kind of baby step toward proving that the new kid in town was cool. After sitting on the sidelines for a while watching the basketball jocks impress the girls with their shooting, I decided that following suit might be my ticket to acceptance.

In reality, the odds that I would make a shot from even six inches away were poor at best. Still, maybe I'd get lucky and heads would swivel in my direction.

I picked up a loose basketball, dribbled a few times, and took a shot. It hit the rim and bounced at a right angle away from me. I jogged over, grabbed the ball again and took another shot. Nothing but net! Unfortunately, it was the part of the net under the rim, which does not count for anything except embarrassment. A third attempt only confirmed to onlookers that I was not a Lebron James in the making.

There was no point in trying to improve my shooting percentage tonight. Rolling the ball away, I walked back toward the sideline and plopped down on the bench. My first attempt to prove that I was somebody had just gone up in flames.

A few minutes later, the basketball jocks were choosing up sides for a quick game. I noticed a player sidle up to one of the team captains and whisper something in his ear. It was obvious that some players hadn't noticed my foray onto the court a few minutes earlier and were uncertain of my basketball skills. The captain, on the other hand, had caught sight of my pathetic attempts to make a basket. Turning back to the player, he sneered and delivered his verdict: "He ain't nothin'."

Although the team captain was talking about my prowess on the basketball court, he might as well have been talking about the way I felt about myself in general. No, I didn't go around telling people that the average cockroach was of infinitely greater value than me. But deep down inside, the sense that I would never live up to others' expectations constantly gnawed at my psyche.

I'd started at Wisconsin Academy in January. Frigid winds blew across the exposed campus, chilling students and faculty to the core. I'd gotten a student job with the maintenance department, but it hadn't lasted long. Personal responsibility had yet to become a strong trait, and an increasing fondness for sleep often found me still in bed when I was supposed to be shoveling sidewalks.

Obsession and anxiety had taken a back seat during this time; I was too busy trying to be accepted to count and worry, at least on a conscious level. My guess is that I was counting steps and clicking my teeth, but the distractions of my current pursuits kept this all below the surface.

A few weeks into what would turn out to be a mere four months spent at Wisconsin Academy, I'd finally found my peer group. Unfortunately, my new friends turned out to share my lack of enthusiasm for anything that resembled academic accountability. Chad was a muscle-bound tough guy from Milwaukee whose demeanor could actually be quite tender. Much as Fonzie discovered in *Happy Days*, this combination was astonishingly effective in drawing good-looking girls to his side. Chad's stepfather, however, wanted little to do with him, and Chad stayed away from home as much as possible. I don't know who was paying Chad's tuition, but boarding school was an oddly good fit for him. Still, much of what I learned about successfully breaking the school's strict rules came as a result of Chad's tutelage.

Lars was another force for ill in my new environs. Ironically, he'd been kicked out of the very school that I'd just left after he'd been caught shoplifting. Lars turned up on campus a few days after my arrival. He immediately got down to the business of plotting various misdeeds.

Since other peer groups and cliques had shown no inclination to recruit my friendship, I chose the path of least resistance and cast my lot with the lawless ones. Chad, Lars, and a few other rebels—male and female— had welcomed me with open arms. Well, at least they hadn't told me to stop hanging around. Slowly but surely, I grew to be accepted by these bad kids with surprisingly good hearts.

One of them was Katie. The fact that she dabbled in a variety of contraband disturbed me, but her fair skin and dark brown eyes overrode my common sense. Add to that the fact that she'd responded positively to a couple of my overtures, and I was hooked. There was a problem though: Katie was still partially hooked on Danny. She made it clear that she'd soon make up her mind regarding which relational road to embark upon. My stomach was in knots for a couple of weeks until she announced her decision: she'd give it a shot with me.

"Unhealthy" would be understating the direction our relationship took over the next few weeks. I was thrilled to have an attractive female paying attention to me, but it came at a price. Katie's parents were unhappily married and on the verge of divorce, and my new girlfriend seemed bent on acting out a lot of her pain. At first it was exciting to sneak around campus after dark and meet up with her, even when the snow was three feet deep and the temperature hovered well below the freezing mark. Still, I was smitten and would do anything to retain Katie's affection.

One night as we walked back together from evening recreational time at the gym, Katie noticed the school principal, Mr. Kinderson, following close behind. Truth be told, we weren't even supposed to be seen together, since we'd been placed on "social," the penalty for having been caught in some kind of public display of affection. But I'd already caught the rebel spirit possessed by Katie and my other newfound renegade friends, so strolling hand-in-hand down the sidewalk in front of the principal seemed fully in character.

As it turned out, Katie wanted to paint a fuller picture of rebellion. "Let's *really* give him something to talk about," she whispered to me. Following her lead, a couple of seconds later found us kissing madly under the outdoor light affixed to the nearest end of the girls' dormitory.

Mr. Kinderson stared in disbelief for a few seconds, then called out, "Randy, meet me in my office *right now!*"

Mission accomplished.

The poet Robert Frost said, "A mother takes twenty years to make a man of her boy, and another woman makes a fool of him in twenty minutes." If only I could place all blame on Katie, but alas, I was a willing accomplice. Besides, at least I was turning heads. Wasn't a bad reputation better than *no* reputation?

I sat across the desk from Mr. Kinderson as he dialed my parents' phone number. I have no recollection of what

[69]

the man actually said to them, but it all ended with his announcement that the school's administrative committee would decide the following day exactly what punishment Katie and I would receive. In the end, it was decided that extending the amount of time Katie and I were to not see or speak to each other would suffice for this particular infraction. Had they known what lay ahead, a different verdict would have been reached.

Academically, I was failing badly. Why take school seriously when there were so many other interesting ways to spend time? It's hard to know exactly why obsessive-compulsive disorder was not interfering with my daily life at this time, but a focus on mischief-making may have played a "helpful" distracting role.

Still technically attached to Katie yet banned from being with her, I used my newfound spare time to get into more trouble. The first of several escapades involved Lars and I strolling off-campus without permission (which we wouldn't have been granted) early on a Sunday morning. As soon as we were out of sight of the academy and its weekend on-duty staff members, we stuck out our thumbs. Our hitchhiking destination was Devil's Lake, a recreational area with not only a lake but substantial climbing boulders as well. It was over an hour before the first vehicle took a gamble on giving us a lift. Devil's Lake was about sixty miles from Wisconsin Academy, but we didn't get there until about noon.

"So, whad'ya wanna do?" Lars asked, surveying the state park.

"Well, we didn't bring anything to swim in, so that's out. Besides, it's still way too cold to go into the lake," I added, nodding toward the nearby icy-cold body of water.

"Yeah. Well, I guess we could climb around on some of these rocks," Lars said.

I joined him for a few minutes, and then he suggested we split up for a while. That was fine with me. I never asked, but I'm pretty sure Lars wanted to take a few swallows of the Southern Comfort that he'd likely brought along with him. I knew from previous encounters that Lars had sewn custom pockets into the lining of his jacket for the sole purpose of shoplifting. I was fairly confident that he presently had some form of illegal substance hidden in those same pockets. Even though my reputation as a miscreant had grown substantially since arriving at Wisconsin Academy, my buddies seemed generally to understand that I was not interested in alcohol or drugs. In some weird way, Lars was honoring my scruples. He also probably didn't want to take the risk of being exposed should I later be interrogated regarding our whereabouts and activities that day.

When Lars and I joined up again a while later, he was pretty jovial. On the other hand, I'd found little to do at Devil's Lake. It's not as if we'd packed in a tent and canoe, or even a decent picnic lunch. I was ready to thumb a ride back to the school. When we got back, Lars and I strolled across campus and into the dining hall just as if we'd been there all day long.

Since our escape to Devil's Lake had turned out well, why not push the illicit adventure envelope a little further?

"I heard Jethro Tull is coming to the Arena in a couple of weeks," I mentioned to Lars. Sure wish I could go."

At the time, Jethro Tull was an immensely popular rock band whose lead singer was also a flute player named

Ian Anderson. Jethro Tull albums included "Aqualung" (1971), which features the romantic ballad "Locomotive Breath." Other albums included "Thick as a Brick," (1972), which in reality was just one song lasting 22 minutes and 37 seconds.

Who wouldn't want to take a monumental risk to attend one of their concerts?

"Who says we can't go to that concert?" Lars said, cracking an evil smile. A brief planning session resulted in our most innovative effort yet to break school rules.

The afternoon before the concert, we began putting our plan into motion. Knowing that my dorm room would be checked for occupancy at 10 P.M. that night, I stuffed my bed to resemble a sleeping human form. Since my head would be underneath the covers, I needed to give the room checker an unmistakable signal that the sleeping form was actually me. No problem. I'd already recorded the appropriate groaning sounds on a tape recorder and pushed the play button. All my roommate had to do was secretly plug the device into the wall socket at just the right time. How could we possibly fail?

Very easily, as it turned out. We'd forgotten that the ten o'clock "lights out" was accomplished every night by turning off the electricity to our dorm rooms. Unfortunately, my tape recorder was not battery-powered. When the stuffed bed tactic also failed, our geese were cooked. I don't recall what punishment Lars received, but I was handed a two-week suspension, hardly the outcome my parents had envisioned when they'd dropped me off at Wisconsin Academy.

It's never been easy for me to express emotions. On the

surface, this may seem odd for someone like me, who feels things deeply. But for some of us, giving voice to those feelings presents a serious challenge. This tendency played an especially complicating role in my life as a young person.

As with most families, ours was imperfect. My parents were members of the "greatest generation," a well-deserved label for those Americans who so valiantly rose to the occasion of helping to save the globe from the devilish likes of Adolph Hitler during World War II. But that same generation often learned that the best way to get along was to go along. Not only had the benefits of psychology not found a place in mainstream America, but its value seemed questionable to the average citizen. If they could win a world war, they were certainly capable of dealing with personal problems without resorting to a "shrink." And if that didn't work, well, they could always just ignore the problems. This was undergirded by stigma associated with mental and behavioral health. Normal people just didn't have a use for such ethereal foolishness.

Nobody sets out to teach their children to stuff their emotions. But I'm fairly sure my parents grew up in homes where surviving family dysfunction consumed a lot of emotional energy. Although I never spoke with them about this subject, my strong inclination is that most of their internal strife never found verbal expression. They certainly had no immediate role models from whom they could learn the immense value of sharing feelings.

It's a small step from not sharing emotions to not divulging *anything* about what you're really thinking. A key benefit of this behavior is that it often helps to "keep the peace." Simply put, speaking up might cause a family member to explode in anger or some other unhealthy behavior. Preserving the illusion that all is well within the family or other relational circle is usually not a conscious choice, but it does provide the desired outcome. Why rock the boat by calling out someone's destructive interpersonal behavior?

Did my mom zip her lips around her alcoholic father? Probably. Did my dad ever openly share his feelings about his emotionally unstable father? I have my doubts. I can only assume that they brought their own experiences surrounding emotional inhibition into their own home. Does it matter?

Yes. Obviously, it doesn't mean every parent who's had a rough home life is a bad person for not possessing ideal parenting skills. We simply do well to learn and grow from our observations. Although my parents expressed their devotion to their two sons in various ways, it did not include saying the words "I love you" until later in life. I would be surprised if they heard those words spoken in their own homes as children.

Some readers may be thinking, *Why don't you just suck it up and move on? After all, everybody's got problems.* True, but not everybody is predisposed to anxiety disorders. And my intent here is to suggest that internalizing emotions has a tendency to exacerbate anxiety issues. For example, it's not uncommon for emotional avoidance to play a significant role in the development of agoraphobia.

I've tried to make a conscious effort to create a more open emotional environment in my own home. But since emotional transparency was not in abundant supply growing up, I've fallen a little short despite my good intentions. Thankfully, today's spectrum of therapies that focus on emotions, such as emotion-focused therapy, can provide real benefit in this area.

I can't change the past, but I can share openly with my sons some of my regret, and encourage them to lay the groundwork for an emotionally nurturing environment in their own homes.

Through the years, I've spoken with several other proverbial "baby boomers" whose parents were not inclined toward emotional displays. Their comments resonate with my own experience. When my parents had conflict or other crises, they did not openly discuss such matters. The only memory I have of my father weeping (until late in life) was when Kenny Allred, the local funeral home director and family friend, was killed while driving an ambulance on winding Red Bud Trail. I was still lying in bed when the phone rang early that morning. I heard Dad climb the stairs, go into the adjacent bedroom, and close the old farmhouse door. He then sobbed for several minutes before reopening the door and heading back downstairs.

No, neither Mom nor Dad were comfortable with exposing too much of their deeper selves. I picked up on their way of handling overpowering emotions in particular.*

My two-week suspension from Wisconsin Academy came to an end. For the second time during a very busy tax season, my parents loaded up the station wagon and headed for the academy. Along the way, we stopped at a

---

*Mental suppression is sometimes called "bottling." This behavior is further explored in Chapter 11.

local restaurant for a late lunch. Shortly after ordering, my father suddenly slumped over in the booth, landing his head on my mother's shoulder. I had no idea what was going on, except that Dad was unconscious.

I looked around at the other patrons and asked, "Does anyone here know CPR?" When nobody stepped up, Mom instructed our waitress to phone for an ambulance. Before it arrived, Dad regained consciousness. The good news was that he had apparently not suffered a heart attack. Nevertheless, when the emergency personnel arrived, they loaded him onto a stretcher and placed him into the ambulance. A couple of hours later, professional evaluation provided no definitive diagnosis. The attending physician gave his clearance for our journey to continue, and all went well the rest of the trip.

But the incident scared the daylights out of me. I'm inclined to think that my inability to stay out of trouble helped to push my dad over the stress threshold, resulting in a fainting episode. It was simply too much, added to an already draining tax return preparation schedule. If only it had pushed *me* toward a long-term commitment to better behavior, my boarding school experience might have ended more positively. Unfortunately, common sense was in short supply during this time. Any lessons to be learned wouldn't stick with me before exercising a great deal more bad judgment on my part.

Katie continued what were now obvious attempts to be permanently tossed out of school. She achieved her goal by running away to Madison and spending several days with friends there. She didn't tell me or anyone else her exact whereabouts, which left me in meltdown state and ultimately needing a tranquilizer prescription. A few days later, she phoned and told me where to pick her up. My parents happened to be visiting me that weekend, and I borrowed their car to fetch Katie from a supermarket parking lot.

The following day found my girlfriend headed back home to Illinois, leaving me both lonely and confused. I saw Katie a few more times after that, but it became increasingly clear she had plans in mind that didn't include me.

Not to be rushed into making sensible decisions, Lars and I decided to follow up our successful Devil's Lake excursion with another illicit Sunday trek. Sure, we'd blown the Jethro Tull caper, but the Devil's Lake adventure had worked out just fine.

"Hmmm, Eastgate Mall next Sunday?" I asked when Lars made the proposition.

"Yeah," Lars responded confidently. "We'll thumb a ride just like we did for Devil's Lake, but this time we'll go to the mall in Madison. Danny wants to go too."

Danny, the same guy who'd captured Katie's attention for a season, was a freshman whose missionary parents had died in a car accident in Africa. It appeared that he'd thrown God overboard, maybe because heavenly hands had failed to protect his saintly parents, or perhaps because those same parents had tried too hard to mold him into something he wasn't. Either way, Danny was determined to make sure nobody would have any reason to consider him a proverbial Goody Two-shoes. As for me, the later anxiety symptoms that would soon dramatically curtail such free-spirited travel had yet to appear. I was up for the ill-advised journey.

By noon the following Sunday, we'd managed to catch rides to the mall some thirty miles away. We walked through its elegant doors and into a flagship store. Lars and Danny headed toward separate aisles, leaving me to wander around by myself. Mom and Dad had given me some cash on their last visit, and I found an item I wanted to buy, so I made my purchase. Lars and Danny rejoined me, and we headed out of the store.

We didn't get very far.

A husky voice rang out from just behind us. "Alright, you three can stop right there." We all came to a halt, but I had no idea what was happening. "Head back into the store," the individual instructed. It turned out the gentleman giving the orders was an undercover security officer.

The three of us waited in the store manager's office for a police officer to arrive. Soon we were placed in handcuffs and escorted out of the mall and into a waiting police cruiser.

At the Dane County sheriff's office, an interrogation revealed that we were under suspicion of shoplifting. I suddenly realized what Lars and Danny had been doing while I'd been paying for my merchandise. The goods that Danny had shoplifted were quickly found, along with most of what Lars had taken. But a tie that Lars had placed inside his jacket hadn't been discovered. The moment we were left alone, Lars whispered to me, "Can I put this tie in your bag?" Stupidly, I agreed. Fortunately, the assigned officer neglected to add up the purchases on my receipt, and I remained innocent of any shoplifting charges.

Arrangements were made for Lars and Danny to appear in court sometime in the future. Meanwhile, the three of us spent the rest of Sunday and into the evening locked up in the Dane County Juvenile Detention Center, waiting for our school principal to arrive to transport us back to the academy.

Before he got there, we were treated to supper in the detention center's dining hall. After we finished the awful meal, a resident much larger than any of us suggested that the "new guys" would probably be delighted to do the dishes that evening. As it turned out, he was correct.

The fight we witnessed between one of the incarcerated youth and a supervisor a short time later was entertaining, but not enough to make any of us newcomers wish we could prolong our stay. It was the first time any of us was thrilled to see Mr. Kinderson walk through the door. He'd completed the paperwork necessary for our release, and soon we were cruising down U.S. 151 back toward the school.

After several miles of silence, Mr. Kinderson finally spoke sharply to me. "Randy, you can either withdraw from school tonight, or the administration will take formal action tomorrow to remove you."

I'm not sure if Lars or Danny were given the opportunity to avoid having the word *expelled* scrawled across their permanent academic record, but I was smart enough to realize that I'd been extended a gracious opportunity.

My parents arrived the next day. We packed my belongings into the station wagon and made a final trip from Wisconsin Academy back to Michigan. I'd lasted at the school for a total of four months.

The above incidents reflect only a portion of the nefarious activities in which I was involved during my short stint at the academy. Why such a propensity for trouble? Did at least some of this barrage of misbehavior involve my affection for controlling anxiety by directing my attention elsewhere? It seems likely.

Again, in no way am I suggesting that my psychological issues were the *sole* reason for my actions. Creative by nature, I have never lacked for resourcefulness in the area of mischief. But low self-esteem, combined with creativity, anxiety, and the need to keep the latter under control, can lead to a vast repertoire of surprising behaviors.

When that year's graduation weekend rolled around at Wisconsin Academy, I decided to make an appearance. I cannot recall how I made the trip. It may have been by Greyhound bus, because I didn't have a car that weekend. My buddy Chad was a graduating high school senior, and his beautiful girlfriend, Nancy, was a junior. Both were scheduled to participate in the weekend events.

Nancy and I had become friends in our own right. "I'd really like to get Chad a copy of *The Prophet* by Kahlil Gibran for a graduation present," she informed me. "I saw a leather-bound copy in Madison a while back, but I don't have a way to get there. I'd need to go tonight." Always eager to share my problem-solving skills, I spoke up. "We could hitchhike there," I suggested. By now it was Thursday afternoon, and the goal was to make it back to campus before anyone counted Nancy as missing.

Out beside the highway, I gave Nancy a few pointers on how to look as irresistible as possible. Soon enough, a male driver pulled over and told us to hop in. The man lost no time in surveying Nancy more closely, and by the time we pulled into his motel's parking lot on the outskirts of Madison, he made his pitch.

"So, where you two gonna stay tonight?" he asked, barely hiding his lust. When I told him we'd figure out something, he shared an idea. "Well, you can both stay in my room," he invited with a wicked grin. Then, speaking directly to me, he added, "*You* can sleep in the bathtub." He had a softer landing spot in mind for Nancy.

We declined his invitation and headed back to the roadside. The man shrugged his shoulders and made his way into the motel office.

Eventually, we located the little shop where Nancy had seen the Kahlil Gibran book, and she made her purchase. But the entire episode had taken longer than we'd imagined, and there was no way Nancy would be back in the dormitory on time. Regardless of my presence alongside her, a lovely young woman hitchhiking in the dark of night could end in disaster. We also both knew that returning to the academy now would only be met by Mr. Kinderson's late-night wrath.

Standing near a highway overpass, I noticed a grassy area nearby. I pointed to the spot and said, "Let's go up there and wait until morning." We made our way up the embankment and plopped down in the unmown grass. Eventually, it turned cold, but not as frigid as the greeting that awaited us back at Wisconsin Academy.

When daybreak came, we scurried down the embankment and stuck out our thumbs. Soon, we caught a ride, and within the hour we were back on campus. Nancy made her way over to the girl's dormitory, where she'd shortly learn that she would not be allowed to stay on campus for graduation weekend. To say that Mr. Kinderson was unhappy to see *me* would be an understatement. Spotting me from a distance, he made a beeline in my direction. His "greeting" was short and to the point.

"Randy, you have thirty minutes to get off campus," he spouted angrily, "or I will call the police."

I decided not to put Mr. Kinderson's threat to the test. A short while later found me at the Greyhound bus station, waiting for a ride out of town. I wonder if Chad still has *The Prophet* sitting around somewhere. To be hoped is that he gained some wisdom from it, something that seemed in short supply in my own life at the time.

SIX

SLEEPING AND WANDERING

During my time at Wisconsin Academy I'd become increasingly fatigued.

A few weeks after being removed from the school, I also began experiencing dizziness and other troubling symptoms. A trip to the doctor included a blood test. A couple of days later, my mom answered the phone. The blood test results had come back.

"Randy has a pretty serious case of mononucleosis," the doctor explained. This was hardly good news for my liver, since I'd already had a bout with hepatitis A. The virus initially left me hospitalized for four days.

The only thing I knew about mononucleosis is that it was nicknamed "the kissing disease." I was overwhelmed and not a little frightened. Had my relationship with Katie brought on this illness? But true to form, I did my best to keep my deepest distress well hidden.

At home, Mom included a nasty combination of grape juice and brewer's yeast as part of my recovery regime. I don't know if it helped, but over the course of a few weeks I began feeling much better. I was sleeping less and, while my blood tests would not be totally free of mono for over a year, I was ready for a new adventure. My parents graciously gave me both their blessing, along with airfare, for a trip to Puerto Rico with my former academy roommate. Haitian by birth, Guito had been adopted by an individual in San Juan, Puerto Rico. Somewhere along the way, Guito had met some Seventh-day Adventist tourists, who encouraged him to attend Wisconsin Academy. His adoptive parent, however, refused to pay for a religious boarding education, and a caring couple in Mayaguez stepped up to provide tuition assistance.

The ten-day Puerto Rican adventure was fun, and it whetted my appetite for more travel. So instead of flying directly back home, I decided to change my ticket and stop in several cities along the way.

When the plane landed in Miami, I grabbed my guitar and suitcase and made my way toward the airport exit. I figured taking a bus downtown should put me in proximity to a hotel, where I'd stay for the night.

"Where ya from?" a hippie-looking young man asked as the city bus bounced along.

"Michigan."

"Got a place to stay?"

"Not yet. I'm gonna try and find something downtown," I responded.

The hippie looked back and said, "You might have trouble with that. The Democratic Convention starts tomorrow night, and all the hotels are probably booked."

With no interest in politics, I didn't even really know what comprised a political convention. This was 1972, and I'd heard something about George McGovern, who seemed pretty cool for a balding, middle-aged politician. But beyond that, I couldn't care less.

"Man, you know what you oughta do?" asked the hippie. "You oughta just camp out with the rest of us demonstrators in Flamingo Park. It's across from the convention center."

Why not? As the bus ground to a halt near the Miami Beach Convention Center, I could hardly believe my eyes. The adjacent park looked like Woodstock South. Hippies and thousands of others milled around in the humid Florida night. It didn't take long for me to realize that for many, illicit drug activity was more a motivation for showing up than making sure the delegates across the street did the right thing.

"You're welcome to crash right here with me," the hippie offered. I set down my stuff and tried to get comfortable. It was already late, but sleep wouldn't come. There were too many lights and too much activity, even at this hour. Around midnight, I gave up. Quietly, I gathered my things and slipped away from the park.

"Do you know of any place I might be able to get a cheap room tonight?" I asked the driver as I swung onto another city bus.

"Well, maybe the YMCA. You could try, at least."

A few minutes later, I stood in front of the huge, dingy-looking facility. I stepped inside and up to the counter. They did indeed have a room available, and soon I found myself lying on the sagging mattress, strumming my guitar. For a while now I'd been having trouble falling asleep at night, and playing my guitar seemed to get the melatonin flowing.

Before I go to sleep, I'd better go use the community

restroom, I told myself. I made my way down the corridor. That's when another thought entered my mind: *Is that man following me?*

Out of the corner of my eye I'd noticed a large African-American man behind me. When he followed me into the restroom, I was pretty sure it wasn't just because he had to pee.

"Hey, I been watchin' you through your window," he told me.

I knew I should've closed the blinds.

He came right to the point. "Wanna have sex?"

Such an invitation I had not received prior to this incident, but it didn't take long for me to formulate a response.

"No."

The man huffed, and said, "Whatsa matter—you chicken?"

Nodding in the affirmative seemed the quickest way to resolve the situation. With that, I returned to my room, packed my things, and headed back outside into the balmy night.

Miami Beach wasn't everything it was cracked up to be, at least not in my affordability range. My restlessness and wandering ways would next find me spending a couple of days with family acquaintances in Orlando, then moving on to Atlanta. That's where my deep-seated fear of making God mad would once again rise to the surface and work to my long-term best interest.

While in San Juan, I'd met Guito's friend Mark. Mark's mom held a management position at the Peachtree Hotel in downtown Atlanta. "If you're ever in town, be sure and stop by," he'd told me. Mark had no idea it would be so soon after our initial meeting.

When a bus at the airport came along marked "Peachtree Street," I figured it would at least take me in the right direction. Just to be sure, I asked the driver if he'd let me know when we got to the Peachtree Hotel. I sat patiently in the back of the bus and watched the lights of Atlanta grow brighter and brighter. When I saw a Peachtree Street sign, I figured we must be getting close. But an introvert often hesitates to speak up when he or she ought to, and my heart sank as I began noticing that we were leaving downtown Atlanta. Finally mustering my courage, I called out, "Will we be getting to the Peachtree Hotel pretty soon?"

The bus driver looked in his rearview mirror at me. "Are you still here?" he asked in disbelief. How he'd managed to miss me I don't know; I was the only person left on the bus!

"We passed the Peachtree Hotel way back there," he informed me. "Now you'll have to wait until I do the whole route one more time."

Atlanta is a lovely town, but if I never again ride on one of its transit buses, it will be much too soon.

Mark hadn't given me his home address, so inside the Peachtree Hotel I asked if they had an employee by the last name of Warfield. Soon Mrs. Warfield met me in the lobby and I explained that I'd met her son a few days earlier in Puerto Rico. The woman made a phone call to Mark whom, from our conversation back in San Juan, I knew should be back in Atlanta by now. Their apartment was within walking distance, and a few minutes later, he strolled into the hotel lobby. "Hey, man, great to see you again!" he said warmly. We chatted for a few minutes, and then Mark led me back to the apartment.

"This is great!" Mark said as I set down my guitar and suitcase. "I've been helping to get a new radio station up and running here in Atlanta, and tonight we're having a celebration party! You'll have a great time. Plenty of booze and other 'goodies'."

Just my luck. I seemed to be drawn to well-meaning druggies like a rainbow trout is drawn to a fish ladder. Sure, I wanted to be viewed as a cool and hip dude, but I also still clung to certain of my Seventh-day Adventist beliefs. The tension that existed between my bad-boy persona and my inner good-boy tenets was surfacing again, just as it had back at Wisconsin Academy. Complicating matters was the fact that this was Friday, and the Sabbath I still tried to observe began at sunset, just a little while after the radio station party would be getting into full swing. Just how much of my spiritual devotion was rooted in an authentic, loving relationship with God, and how much was merely an obsession with not wanting to anger Him may never be known.

Suddenly, I realized that I might have a creative way to please both God and man.

"What time did you say the party starts?" I asked Mark.

"6:30."

Bingo! Sunset wasn't until 7:30! I didn't yet know how I'd escape when the time came, but I was determined to make an appearance at the den of iniquity before high-tailing it out of there to keep my Sabbath holy.

I rode with Mark and his friends to the party, where spirits were high indeed. I did my best to fit in, but it was especially difficult because I didn't know anybody besides Mark.

"Hey, Randy," Mark said a few minutes later as he walked in my direction. "Me and a couple of other guys are gonna go buy some weed. Wanna come along?"

God's favor had just rested upon me.

"Um, no, you guys just go ahead," I said, trying to conceal any look of glee that may have crossed my face. "But thanks."

Mark nodded. With that, he and two of his buddies left the room. As soon as they were out of sight, I headed for the closest exit. I'd have to walk several miles back into downtown Atlanta. With the remnants of mononucleosis still circulating through my worn-down system, I began the trek. I knew Mark's mom was heading out of town for the weekend, and somehow, I'd have to get into their apartment to grab my guitar and clothes. From there, I'd need to thumb a ride to the airport; my trip cash was down to coinage.

A couple of hours later, I'd finally made my way into the Peachtree Street district. I was exhausted but still had some goals to accomplish. So did the girl walking straight toward me from the opposite direction. She blocked my path, infringed upon my personal space, and started rubbing my stomach. "I need a little cash," she said with a hopeful smile. "Anything will help."

The belly rub was a nice touch, but I told her I was broke. Our relationship ended quickly. I never was a panhandler's mother lode.

At last I came to my hosts' apartment building, which was an older brick structure. Incredibly, Mark's mom was just walking up to the building. I told her I needed to get my things because I was heading out of town. The woman herself was in a rush, so she didn't ask too many questions. Within a few minutes, I'd gathered my belongings and headed back out onto Peachtree Street.

Hartsfield International Airport wasn't anywhere within walking distance, so I knew my only option was hitchhiking. By now it was well into Friday evening. I knew which freeway went in the direction of the airport, but I didn't know how to get to the freeway. Holding a suitcase in one hand and my guitar in the other, I approached an older African-American gentleman loitering just off the sidewalk in a storefront entryway. He told me how to get to a nearby embankment I could sidle down and end up smack on the edge of the freeway. Then he added this ominous warning: "I wouldn't go down there this time of night. It's real dangerous."

I recalled reading about a serial killer wandering around Atlanta at this particular time. But I was out of options—I had less than a dollar in my pocket. What I did have, though, was an airline ticket home. The only thing standing between me and takeoff were a few dimly lit freeway miles.

"Well, thanks for the advice," I replied, "but I really need to get to the airport." With that, I turned and began walking toward the embankment.

That's when a grizzled old man stopped me. Pointing at the guitar case I held, he said, "Ya wanna sell that there guitar?"

Taken aback, I didn't know quite what to say. After a few seconds, though, I realized the magnitude of the proposal on the table. "Well, uh, normally I wouldn't be interested in selling it, but I sorta need some cash right now," I told the old man.

"I unnerstand," he said. "So do ya wanna sell it?"

"Well, I guess so."

"How much?" he asked. I have no recollection of the old man asking to see the instrument, although he may have.

I gave him a price and he nodded. Suddenly, he bent over, pulled outward on one of his socks and reached deep into it with his other hand. I watched in astonishment as he pulled out quarter after quarter until the agreed-upon price lay piled in my cupped hands. There was not one paper bill in the entire cache. The old man picked up my guitar and moseyed on down the street. He'd gotten a good deal, but so had I.

It was almost midnight in Atlanta. With plenty of quarters in my pocket, I found a pay phone and called for a taxi to take me to the airport. A few hours later I was airborne, homeward bound.

Do angels grow whiskers, store quarters in their socks, and dabble in used musical instruments? Harps, maybe, but a Sears Silvertone guitar that barely held its tune and was sheer misery to play? Did a serial killer miss his chance with me that night? Was the chain of events that took me safely home coincidence, providence, or perhaps a combination of both? Four decades of hindsight have convinced me that I was not abandoned, that Someone was in fact watching over me. But if that were true, why stop there? Couldn't that same "Higher Power" gaze just a few years into the future and stave off the psychological distress around which my life would soon revolve?

I can speculate until the proverbial cows come home,

but I've chosen to focus on what actually took place rather than wallow in and wonder about what *didn't* happen.

My buddy Chad and I stayed friends after my departure from Wisconsin Academy and his graduation. Not given to the college scene, Chad found creative ways to fill his wallet, some of them even legal. Eventually, he landed gainful employment as a dishwasher-waiter at the stately Pfister Hotel in downtown Milwaukee. "You oughta come here and work too," he urged. "I'm pretty sure you could get a job in the same area I'm working in." Since I didn't have anything steady going on in the way of employment, the idea intrigued me.

A couple of weeks later, I found myself in the Land of Ten Thousand Breweries. I checked out the Pfister one night when my pal was on duty. Chad looked downright respectable in his hotel duds, but was this the place for me? I'd have to think about it.

Saint Patrick's Day was that week, and Chad had planned an evening out with a couple of his friends who lived in Milwaukee. "We're gonna go to a bar and drink green beer!" he said with a grin. Since my religious roots still ran deep in their own twisted way, the idea of a night of drinking beer, green or otherwise, wasn't too appealing. Still, I needed friends. The last thing I wanted to do was tell Chad that his mentee in misbehavior was actually some kind of Jesus freak! But beyond that, there was the haunting sense that drinking alcohol might cause me to lose control in some way. No, I couldn't take that risk. The whole "designated driver" thing was still years ahead, so that wasn't on my radar. Somehow I'd figure out how to blend in without coming off as a saint in training.

The big night arrived, and we took a booth in the bar recommended for the festivities. "We're all gonna get green beer, r-i-i-ght?" one of Chad's friends said with a knowing smile.

As it turned out, he didn't know as much as he thought. I don't recall any stinging barbs as my three compatriots sipped on their mugs of green beverage while I enjoyed my soft drink. Maybe they knew better than to pick on one of Chad's out-of-town guests, I don't know. The important thing is that I hadn't made God mad, and alcohol coursing through my veins wouldn't cause me to do something irrational in Beertown. After all, I had to keep everything under control.

As for the Pfister gig, I took a pass. I'm not sure what I missed, but plenty of surprises—and ample agony—lay just ahead.

SEVEN

ARRESTING EVENTS

"You have the right to remain silent . . ." Before that evening, the only time I'd heard those words were on TV, and they certainly hadn't been directed at me. But a quick learner I was not. A few hours in the Dane County Juvenile Detention Center had fallen short as an adequate deterrent. An actual arrest would be required to nudge me in a less trouble-making direction.

In my quest for coolness, my *modus operandi* was to foster an appearance of evil without actually dipping too deeply into it. Take marijuana, for example. I was not a proponent of the stuff—I just liked to flirt with the idea of being unlawful. So I stuffed a little container full of supposed weed (I had no way of knowing if it was real, since I'd not personally tried it) that I'd gotten hold of somewhere into the crevasse between the upper and lower portions of my Lincoln Continental's rear seat. *That should put me sufficiently at risk,* I reasoned. Just to be sure that I was living on the edge, I found an old whiskey bottle beside the road and created a concoction that looked and smelled a little bit like the real thing. I tossed it under my driver's seat. Everything was in place to allow me to look and feel like a bad boy without actually yielding control to mind-altering substances. Avoiding a loss of control had become an all-absorbing quest—but from what?

Fear of losing control is a common theme in the lives of many who suffer from anxiety disorders. The obsessive-compulsive personality seems especially vulnerable to such thinking. We've been known to worry about suddenly "going crazy" and driving into opposing traffic or running through the church sanctuary stark naked. More subtle versions find us worrying about whether the *thunk* we just heard underneath our vehicle was the result of striking someone walking along the dark roadway, so we turn around just to be sure it wasn't. I've never headed into oncoming traffic or stripped down in church, but I did once turn around to see if I'd struck someone on Mapleville Road. No body was discovered. On the lighter side, during one therapy session, I told the psychologist that I'd been so sick with a virus all week that I'd lost my current fear that I might jump from my car into an adjacent river. I simply didn't have the energy to worry about it. We both had a good laugh.

"Intrusive thoughts" are what therapists call the thoughts we wish would keep their distance from our own mind. As mentioned above, I've had these kinds of thoughts. More accurately, I've tried to resist such streams of consciousness. So that pretty much seals the deal, right? I'm a credentialed wacko.

Not so fast. In *The Man Who Couldn't Stop*, David Adam points out that "survey after survey shows that about nine in ten people admit they experience intrusive thoughts that distress, bewilder, shock, and perplex them. *Most people have thoughts about driving their car off the road.* A third of us say we have thoughts of grabbing money. More than four in ten get an urge to jump from a high place, an impulse so common that it has its own scientific name: the high-place phenomenon. Half of all women and eight out of ten men have thoughts of strangers in the nude, while half of all people cannot help but think of sex acts they consider 'disgusting'. Intrusive thoughts are everywhere [italics mine]."[1]

Adam tells of an intriguing study of intrusive thoughts by South African-born psychologist Stanley Rachman and his Sri Lankan colleague Padmal de Silva:

> "When the psychologists wrote down the weird thoughts harvested from the minds of their OCD patients and those from their 'normal' associates on index cards, and mixed the cards up, even their most experienced clinical colleagues could not correctly distinguish which thoughts came from the damaged minds of patients considered mentally ill and which came from the highly respected people they worked and socialized with."[2]

At least in the matter of weird thoughts, it seems that I'm not so out of the mainstream after all. That's kind of a scary thought—or maybe not.

"Check this out!" I told my buddy Tom one summer evening. Our parents wouldn't let us own guns, so I did the next-best thing: I purchased a .22-caliber "starter pistol," the kind coaches and others use to signal the start of a race. Even though they didn't take real bullets, in

Michigan at that time it was illegal for someone under 21 to own one. I hadn't quite reached that age, but I wasn't worried. On the off chance that I did get caught, what kind of police officer would bother booking a 19-year-old kid for carrying a starter pistol?

"Pretty cool," Tom said, checking out the "weapon." I handed it to him, and he shot off a couple of blanks.

"Hey," Tom said, changing the subject, "my older brother, Donnie, is in the hospital in South Bend. Let's take your Lincoln down there, and I'll run in and see him. We can goof around along the way."

"Goofing around" with Tom was nothing new. Our affection for wacky-but-usually-not-very-dangerous activities spanned a large spectrum. Tom had been sporting a full beard for some time, and his Native American heritage now left him looking uncannily like Fidel Castro (I know Castro isn't Native American—cut me some cultural slack here, OK?). One of my fondest memories of our "Tom-foolery" was the night my buddy dressed in combat fatigues, complete with hat, which strongly resembled Fidel's typical attire. Just before we hit the road, I dashed into Johnson's News Lobby and bought a bubblegum cigar to complete the Castro look. From there, we drove my Lincoln around town, stopping next to cars at stoplights and freaking out drivers who spotted the communist dictator sitting in the front passenger seat of my car. Later reflection undoubtedly left our victims wondering what Fidel Castro was doing in their town and why there was no smoke coming from his stogie.

But the current night's adventure was destined to top all. The fact that I had no valid license plates on my vehicle was not really a problem. I had a couple of old

Tennessee license plates out in the barn, so I'd just covered up the bare places on my vehicle's front and rear bumpers with them. After all, we were only going to be traveling to South Bend and back. What could go wrong? What kind of police officer would bother to ticket a couple of broke teenagers just out having a little fun?

With everything ready, I tossed the starter pistol onto the front seat and cranked the engine. Soon our entire carload full of contraband was rolling smoothly down highway U.S. 31 toward South Bend, Indiana.

Just north of Niles, Michigan, an idea struck me. "Hey, Tom, just for fun, let's pretend like you're carjacking me! You know, take the starter pistol and point it at my head as we drive along! Ha, ha!"

"Ha, ha!" Tom said. "That's a good one. That ought to really freak out the drivers coming toward us! Ha, ha!" With that he picked up the starter pistol, rested his left arm on the back of the front seat, and pointed the item toward my head.

It can sometimes be difficult to discern the difference between creative expression and world-class lunacy. This was not one of those times. Stupidity was flowing with the force of Niagara Falls.

Just south of Niles I glanced in my rearview mirror. The familiar single rotating light perched atop a Michigan State Police car signaled that my evaluation of what might prompt action from law enforcement had been wrong. I pulled over and stopped directly opposite the local K-Mart. Another patrol car pulled in behind the first one, followed by yet another. My fascination turned to consternation when a state police officer approached with revolver drawn. "Slide out of the car this way and

keep your hands where I can see them," he command-
ed. A minute or so later found both Tom and I hunched
over my car's trunk, our hands behind our backs. An officer slapped a pair of silver handcuffs onto Tom's wrists,
while mine were secured with a plastic zip tie.

By now, the entire scene was providing quite a show
for passersby, some of whom may have been members
of Tom's home church, located right there in Niles. He'd
just been approved to serve as a church deacon, and this
episode would do little to enhance his résumé.

The police officers thoroughly searched the car, turning up the fake bottle of whiskey and the starter pistol.
My guess is that they were pretty disappointed, but they
still had enough to make our life miserable. Providential-
ly (I believe), the little bottle containing the weed was
missed as the officer's hand somehow swept through that
very area without discovering it.

Our Miranda rights were delivered enroute to the local
state police headquarters, where Tom and I were hand-
cuffed to each other through a steel wall-mounted hoop.
Of course, the license plates were determined to be fake,
which added to the growing list of our trespasses. In the
end, I was charged with driving with an open container of
alcohol (a lab test, of course, would have revealed otherwise, but I didn't think of requesting one soon enough),
illegal possession of a starter pistol (yeah, really), and the
license plate fiasco. We were informed that a driver in the
opposite lane had phoned in her concern that someone
was being carjacked—imagine that. A couple of hours
later, we were released into the custody of my beleaguered CPA father, along with a document announcing
our court date.

At our court appearance, the judge informed us that our youth leader, whose day job was that of probation officer, had personally phoned him on our behalf. Mr. Lyle had told the judge that we were basically "good kids," and that seemed to hold some sway. In the end, I received a fine, and we were both placed on ninety days' probation.

How could someone so prone to panic exhibit this kind of senseless behavior, which in practical terms was nothing short of baiting the state police? Didn't I have even an inkling that this could only turn out badly? Maybe I did. But in my case, there may have been another reason. For a teenager with low self-esteem, any attention can seem better than no attention. In fact, low self-esteem is common to many of us who battle anxiety disorders. So does a propensity for panic lead to low self-esteem, or is it the other way around? My guess is that it's neither. I think it's simply part of a bevy of characteristics that many folks, though certainly not all, such as myself, share in common. One of these is a high level of creativity, ironically very often accompanied by low self-esteem. For example, one of the most talented illustrators I know, whose work has appeared in such publications as *Rolling Stone*, often told me how unspecial she considered herself to be. Given her abilities, I find it astonishing, yet at the same time not surprising.

I'm grateful that therapy and peer affirmation through the years have helped me correct course along these lines. While it's unlikely that my self-appreciation will ever rise to the level of considering myself God's "gift" to anything (at least, I hope not), I do now celebrate the person I've become, mental illness and all. While anxiety disorders can still sometimes be a royal pain in the brain,

I trust that a growing sense of self-acceptance is a step in the right direction.

"And now it's time for another story of drama and human condition—a tale well designed to keep you in . . . *Anxiety!*"[3] That's how the comedy duo Bob and Ray introduced their parody of *"Suspense,"* a classic radio show of yesteryear. Although the funny men replaced the word *suspense* with *anxiety,* both terms have their place in my personal history. I could never quite predict how and when troubling symptoms would rise to the surface, or how they might manifest themselves.

It reminds me of my years-long battle with groundhogs. Our home in Maryland sits on a ridge overlooking portions of West Virginia, western Maryland, and Pennsylvania. This makes for gorgeous sunsets, but the limestone embankments that cascade behind our house are a groundhog's dream come true.

This much I learned early on: Don't think you can fill in the critter's tunnel entrance and expect that you've made any progress. Not even pouring a concrete slab over its hole means diddly squat to a groundhog. Short of taking drastic measures, the abominable rascal will simply reroute itself, soon to pop its head up through nearby soil and sport a toothy grin, which is its way of saying, "Nice try, sucker."

Yeah, that's what trying to repress anxiety can seem like.

So just what is anxiety, really? When it comes to answering that question there's a fair amount of disagreement among psychologists. In *Living With Anxiety,* by Drs. Bob Montgomery and Laurel Morris, we find some

help. Montgomery and Morris suggest this working definition: "Anxiety is an unpleasant state that includes

▶ negative emotions (for example, you feel fearful,
nervous, jittery, distressed, or upset)

▶ expecting unpleasant or threatening events, inside
or outside yourself, but seeing them as unpredictable and out of your control

▶ shifts in your attention to focus needlessly on the
possible threats and your reactions to them."[4]

The authors provide some intriguing insight into anxiety and various cultures:

Researchers have found that something like anxiety
exists in most, if not all other cultures and that the
nature of the anxiety process tends to reflect the
characteristics of each culture. For example, Chinese
people may complain of a problem called *pa-leng*,
an apparently exaggerated fear of losing body
heat, which they believe results from an imbalance
between the life forces, *yin* and *yang*. Iranians may
complain of "heart distress," describing physical
symptoms centering on the heart but bearing a strong
resemblance to a Western panic attack. There are
well-documented folk magic rituals in a number of
cultures, such as voodoo dolls in the Caribbean and
"pointing the bone" among Australian Aborigines,
which seem to involve scaring the victim to death
by causing an intolerably high level of anxiety.

Using standard checklists of anxiety symptoms,
researchers have found similar levels of anxiety

in different cultures. Which symptoms people complained of, how they explained the symptoms to themselves and, therefore, what was effective help for them varied from culture to culture. But anxiety itself seems to be a universal and therefore normal part of being human.[5]

Other research, however, suggests that one country in particular may indeed deserve the grand prize for Most Anxious Nation. Writer and blogger Ruth Whipmann points out, "Despite being the richest nation on earth, the United States is, according to the World Health Organization, by a wide margin, also the most anxious, with nearly a third of Americans likely to suffer from an anxiety problem in their lifetime. America's precocious levels of anxiety are not just happening in spite of the great national happiness rat race, but also perhaps, because of it."[6]

So in the matter of which global arena is the most anxious, the research seems to send a mixed message. Either way, I don't advocate voodoo or "pointing the bone" for relief, but I suppose there is something comforting in knowing that anxiety exists in other perfectly normal people.

The times when my mental anguish seemed to go underground were welcome respites, yet proved temporary. Sooner or later, anxiety reared its uglier-than-a-groundhog's head. But I didn't know much about groundhogs or repressed emotions back then, so I went about life doing whatever it took to get by. A girlfriend here, a part-time job there—add a Fiat 850 Sports Spider convertible to the mix, and there wasn't a lot of time left to click my teeth and count my steps, at least not at a conscious level.

During those years, I dabbled as a student at four different high schools. Officially, I am a graduate of Lakeshore High School in Stevensville, Michigan. That's because their adult education coordinator had somehow gotten hold of my name and called me on the phone one day. I was a dropout at the time.

"According to the records I have, you need only a couple of classes to graduate, Randy. I'll tell you in confidence that our Adult Ed classes are usually pretty easy. I'm encouraging you to enroll."

Easy sounded good, so I signed up. The classes were held evenings, and the coordinator was right—the course content wasn't exactly academically robust. For example, one of my classes was a foray into the world of international cuisine, and my final project involved baking something called flan, a Mexican custard. This was a far cry from the usual high-school fare of biology and trigonometry, but somehow in the end, a bona fide high school degree soon appeared in my mailbox. I'd flanned my way to academic success!

Sarah and I had now parted ways, and my buddy Tom and I often commiserated at length about our romantic woes. Tom had been my best friend since sixth grade and lived over on Huckleberry Road, just a couple of miles from my house. We shared much in common; in particular, our conviction that academic excellence was a far less worthy pursuit than chasing girls.

But something new (or renewed) was now regularly making its way onto the landscape of my behavioral horizon. I was beginning to experience a high level of discomfort when driving alone, especially after dark. Shades of panic began to rise whenever I needed to travel outside of my geographical comfort zone, the boundaries of which seemed to be diminishing week by week. I fought the symptoms, but just as with those first couple of panic attacks in Wisconsin and Chicago, resistance only seemed to make matters worse. As usual, when the attacks hit, my quickening heart rate was accompanied by dizziness and a narrowing field of vision. Earlier diagnoses had left me uncertain regarding the actual source of these distressing symptoms. All I knew was that whenever they began to creep over me, I needed to quickly return to a safe person or place lest I die in my car, away from all that was familiar.

Clearly, I needed help, so I began seeing a clinical psychologist. Dr. Baker's expertise was in the area of "talk" or "insight" therapy. I gained quite a bit of helpful insight, much of which centered on the way I'd been brought up. Every session delivered a temporary fix of relative peace and a measure of hope that someday things would be better. But progress was slow, and I stood on the precipice of a deep, dark chasm from which I would not soon escape.

If obtaining a high-school diploma seemed unlikely, securing a college degree was surely downright impossible. By this time, I'd tried my hand at several different unskilled jobs— mowing cemetery lawns, top-dressing golf course putting greens, and painting apartments. I'd also dabbled in a foliage growing and distribution enterprise, having constructed two polyethylene greenhouses behind the barn on the family property.

At the same time, I was taking an occasional college

class at the local university. Not that I seriously thought I'd one day earn a degree. Still, in the pursuit of a clear-cut vocational future, I was going nowhere in high gear. Maybe the right college course would dredge up some kind of latent career passion.

One of the first required classes was Psychology 101. Secretly nervous in general about anything related to mental health (after all, subject matter might hit too close to home, and that would be insufferable), I nevertheless signed up for the course. *I'll have to take it sooner or later,* I reasoned. *Might as well get it over with.*

During the first week, the professor facilitated a discussion about strange thought patterns in the mentally ill. "For example, some individuals suffer what is called 'phantom limb,' a syndrome in which a person thinks their limb is present even though it may have been amputated," the professor intoned. "Such mind-body self-deception can be highly debilitating in and of itself."

As the discussion continued, I grew increasingly anxious. What if, as a result of learning about various psychological ailments, I began experiencing them myself? I shifted nervously in my seat, until at last I rose and left the room. It was all too much for my susceptible psyche to endure.

I dropped the class. Higher education would have to wait until at least the next semester.

As with so much else, this all sounds absurd even as I write about it. But such concerns were not atypical during those days. In this incident, an undefined sense that I might lose control in some fashion—perhaps of my own mental faculties—proved too overpowering for me to challenge.

An Anxious Kind of Mind

When anxiety or obsession seemed about to overwhelm me, I sometimes arranged to see a physician. Usually, they were not very helpful. I don't blame them. For example, recently, as an editor of a true stories magazine for children, I would not have boatloads of helpful counsel for an adult fiction writer. Similarly, we would be naïve to think that a general practitioner would be an expert in mental health issues. One doc "prescribed" vitamins for my anxiety. The man clearly had no concept that not even a dozen vitamin pills per day would begin to put a dent in my locker full of anguish. Such medical professionals *meant* well, but they didn't help me *get* well.

Back on campus, I eventually signed up for another class: Radio Broadcasting. It took just one day for me to conclude that I was not destined to become the next Charles Kuralt. But one day *was* enough for me to notice a strikingly good-looking female student. The next day found me needing to achieve two goals: drop the class and find out the girl's name.

Since Andrews University is relatively small, it was not uncommon to run into someone I knew around campus. What *was* unusual is that I should show up in the university library. But for whatever reason, that evening found me searching the lofty stacks for a now-forgotten tome. It wasn't a book that caught my eye, however, but two females seated at a nearby study table. I happened to know one of them, but the other didn't seem—wait a minute! Could it be true? I looked more closely and sure enough, the person studying with my friend was the same girl I'd noticed in the radio broadcasting class!

Slowly, I made my way toward the table and spoke to the girl I knew. "Sorry to bother you, but could I see you over here for a minute?" I asked Cindi. She raised an eyebrow but followed me around a corner and out of her friend's sight. I got right to the point.

"Hey, if you don't mind me asking, who is that girl you're studying with?"

Cindi smiled. "Her name is Diana. She just moved here from California. Her parents came here a couple of years ago to work at the university, and she decided to live with them and finish her degree."

My second question was just as forthright. "Does she have a boyfriend?"

"No, I don't think so."

"OK. I want to ask her out for a date."

Cindi didn't say much in response and soon headed back to the study table. I later learned what had taken place there.

"Who was that?" Diana had asked with palpable indifference.

"His name is Randy."

"What did he want?"

"Oh, he wanted to know who you were and if you had a boyfriend. He said he wants to ask you for a date. But he's a real joker; I wouldn't worry about it."

"Yeah, OK."

Diana and I were married on August 12, 1979. She had no idea that my anxious afflictions would become a challenge to both of us.

EIGHT

SHORT-BUS HOMIES

"*YAHRRR!*" Rodney's screams of delight could be heard for blocks.

To this day, I'm not sure how old he actually was. All I really remember is seeing the mentally retarded fellow—a young adult, I think—swinging wildly back and forth on the homemade swing lashed to a massive tree limb in his back yard. His house was just down the street and across from the home where I lived until I was 6 years old.

I was terribly afraid of Rodney—so much so that I tried not to even look at him as he swung and screamed. Whether we'd been "warned" about Rodney by parents and neighbors, I cannot recall. All I know is that I considered the screaming "idiot" to be more dangerous than Jack the Ripper.

Dean's Dairy, a full-service milk-bottling plant, was located just down the street from our house. Inside the facility resided a freezer case filled with all manner of frozen confectionary delights. Getting there, however, meant walking past Rodney's house. Fortunately, I was too young to make the short journey alone. Mom, Dad, a cousin, or somebody else served as bodyguards, should Rodney suddenly leap from his swing and charge me waving a machete.

Of course, Rodney was in no way dangerous. I am not sure what his challenge was—perhaps Down Syndrome. I mention him only because it is my earliest memory of being afraid of a "crazy person," or "idiot," as such were called back in the day. How it happened may be irrelevant. The fact remains that somehow, I'd had planted in my brain that "retards" were to be avoided at all cost. In succeeding years, this developed into a pattern of both mental and physical avoidance of the mentally handicapped. I didn't want to be around them or even think about them. In some irrational way this helped ensure that I wouldn't catch whatever contagion they suffered from.

By the time Diana and I were engaged, I'd yet to completely free myself from such twisted thinking. But with a wedding on the horizon, I needed cash. What I ended up doing was something I could hardly have foreseen. I applied for a job driving mentally handicapped students to and from their educational facility! When I learned that I'd gotten the job, I didn't know whether to laugh or cry, but at least I was facing a deeply buried, though irrational, fear.

As the new bus driver for this group of mentally challenged students, I decided to give it my best shot and make the job as interesting as possible. After all, I would be out on the road several hours a day with nothing to do, with no intelligent person to talk to or kid around with. Just a bus full of "crazies." Oh, they had other names for them—"mentally handicapped" people—but I knew the truth from the beginning: they were nut jobs.

My assigned vehicle was Bus 11-A, known as a "short bus" due to the fact that is wasn't as long when compared to a regular school bus. I pulled up in front of the Blossomland Learning Center. It was my first afternoon on the job, and as I shut off the engine, I looked apprehensively toward the school door.

The first student to walk out was a boy, kind of. His oblong head appeared to be about a size 9, but the rest of his body was a size 8. A girl in a wheelchair followed closely behind. Her hands were twisted, and she was drooling. One by one they came, some limping like wounded ducks, others simply staring aimlessly, spaced out on their medications. I had never seen such an array of unfortunates in my life.

I assumed a casual slump in the driver's seat to hide my uncertainty. As my first passenger got to the bus, I reached over and swung open the door. He was an African-American young adult, and he looked as though he had strolled straight out of a Sunday youth group. He sported a purple velvet suit jacket with polyester slacks just a shade lighter. He walked confidently and stepped onto the bus.

"Hello. My name is James." He spoke with determined emphasis.

He talks! I thought in a state of shock.

"I hope you and me'll be real good friends," he continued. "I ain't like my brother Bobo, who's always sleepin' in and gettin' in fights. No, I'm a lover, not a fighter!" He swaggered toward his seat in the middle of the bus.

A plump white girl with a scarf wrapped tightly around

her head climbed aboard. She stopped next to me, oblivious to several youngsters trying to crowd in behind her.

"Afternoon!" she said in slow, thickened tones. "I'm Barbara, and I'm 26 years old. Do you know what happened on *The Price is Right?*"

"No, I guess not." I didn't immediately sense how that program was relevant to our present situation.

"That woman won a refrigerator, a TV, and a brand-new car! Yes, sir, she did! That was June 14, 1974, it was." She beamed and walked proudly to her seat. A handsome young man strode swiftly toward us, swung onto the bus like an old pro, and landed directly in the seat behind me.

"Mmm—Hello, I'm Tommy," he said. "We had a—mmm—dance this afternoon. I danced with all the girls. "I got—mmm—about five girlfriends." He settled his chin on the handrail that separated us and watched every move I made.

The last one out of the school was a small boy led by his teacher. He had huge Eddie Cantor eyes, and his head moved back and forth like a bobblehead figurine. After he boarded, I pulled the bus door shut, fired up the engine, and started off.

As we bounced away from the school, the picture I had formed of quiet lonely hours on the road rapidly changed. The two-way radio that I had cherished as a last means of communication with the real world had to be turned up full volume before I could hear it over the noisy chatter. And then my passengers simply raised their voices a few decibels and bombarded me with questions.

"You got a wife?" a shout came from the back.

"Not quite yet, but almost," I hollered in return.

"You got a picture of her?" I was harassed into turning the wallet photo of my fiancée over to the group.

"Ohhh, she's pretty!" they echoed.

"I'm gonna marry her!" one of them shouted.

"You can't marry her," I responded defensively. "Our wedding is coming up, and then my wife will already be married." My voice faded as I tried to figure out what I had just said.

As we drove on, I tried to pick up snatches of their conversation.

"You're going *where* tomorrow?" Tommy questioned his seatmate.

"Hawaii. But I'll be back for school on Wednesday."

"Marcus, you can't go to Hawaii tomorrow," scoffed Tommy.

"Why not?"

"Cause I betcha Hawaii's about, oh, 300 miles away from Michigan!"

They are *crazy*, I thought.

At Marcus's home I bid him "Aloha," glanced in my rearview mirror, and wondered what it was really like in their world. On the other hand, did I really want to know?

Still, as the days went by, I found myself becoming curious about specific individuals. I had discovered that the youngster with the big eyes was, in fact, blind. Still, there was a difference in Kenny. He understood what was going on around him. It was almost as though some other sense had replaced the visual perception. He always knew whose stop was next and just exactly where we were on our bus route. How did he do it?

One day on our morning route, after hearing him warn

the other kids that "the bridge is just ahead so we better hang on," I could no longer contain my curiosity.

"Tommy, how come Kenny always knows where we are and whose house is next?"

Tommy, his big chin on the handrail, slowly lifted his head.

"It's simple. He—mmm—hears—a kid get on the bus, then he—mmm—hears that kid talk, then he knows—mmm—who's getting' on next! He got it all figured out!"

"Oh, it *is* simple. Thanks." I felt stupid. But how could a mentally handicapped boy figure all that out? Was he smarter than I had thought? I decided to test him.

"Kenny, would you like to play a game?"

"Yeah! Let's play a game!" he shouted back eagerly.

"OK. You listen to the different sounds I make and then tell me what they are."

"Oh, me and my daddy play this game at home. It's a guessing game!"

"OK. Are you ready?"

"Ready!"

"What's this?" I flipped the overhead flashers on, and the ticking sound began.

"The blinkers!" he shouted without hesitation.

"Good, Kenny!" I felt almost as triumphant as he did.

"Kenny got that one quick!" Tommy said.

A few of the other passengers began to notice what we were doing.

"Now how about this sound? Can you tell me what this is?" I touched the brake pedal lightly a couple of times. Kenny squirmed in his seat. He began to speak and then was silent.

"Try it, Kenny," Tommy pleaded.

"I think—" he began and then stopped.

"Come on, Kenny! You can do it!" Tommy urged.

After several seconds of hesitation, Kenny blurted out, "The brakes!" Sighs of relief floated toward the front of the bus. A cheer came from Marcus, and Tommy patted Kenny on the head.

"Kenny pretty smart! He pretty smart!" But I had one final test.

"Kenny, this is the last one. Now try real hard," I said. I reached down and turned on the windshield wipers.

"What is making that noise?" Everyone grew silent as the wipers swished.

Kenny was confused. He squirmed and said nothing.

"Can you tell me what it is?" I questioned him.

Several passengers leaned forward; others slid to the edge of their seats. Silence. Kenny remained quiet and unsure.

"Come on, Kenny!" Tommy pleaded. "You know— mmm—what that is!"

"Kenny can tell what it is," Marcus informed the bus at large. "Give him a minute."

All the riders now began urging him to listen carefully to the rhythmic sweep of the wiper blades. The only other sound was the muffled grind of the engine.

Kenny's mouth opened and closed without speaking.

"He's just a little boy," Barbara remarked slowly and quietly. I felt the love in her voice.

That did it. Kenny shouted out, "The windshield wipers!" Wild cheers and applause broke throughout Bus 11-A. I breathed a deep sigh of relief.

"You did good, Kenny!" Tommy congratulated him. "I—mmm—knew you could do it!"

"Yeah, nice going, Kenny." I recognized undisguised pride in my voice.

The next day Tommy was perched behind me as usual.

"Hey, Randy! We sure did have—mmm—fun with Kenny yesterday," he said. "I think we make him feel real good. Make you—mmm—feel good too, didn't it?" Tommy spoke again. "You not the same as our last driver. She—mmm—not friendly like you! She not love us like you. You good—mmm—friend, aren't you, Randy?"

How could he say that? What had I done to make him think I was friendly? Then the fog in my brain began to dissipate. Maybe Kenny wasn't the only blind one on the bus after all. If Tommy thought that making up games and giving Kenny a test proved my friendship, what would a real gesture of friendliness mean to them?

"Could I have your attention, please?" I shouted to make myself heard over the roar of the engine and the chatter of my passengers. "I have an announcement to make. Tomorrow is going to be the Bus 11-A Christmas Party. I'll bring cider and donuts for everyone, and we'll pull over at the township park. How does that sound?"

Amid the cheering and excited laughter, I realized that tomorrow I would face my test. Was I really beginning to love this bunch, or was I only playacting?"

Suddenly, something smashed into the windshield. I glanced out the side window and saw a kid laughing gleefully because he had scored a direct hit with his snowball. Then I saw him making fun of my passengers, twisting his body to imitate the handicaps of my crew. An idea struck my mind.

"Tommy, he can't do that to us!" I yelled.

"No! He can't—mmm—do that to us!" he echoed.

I pulled the bus around the next corner and stopped. I reached over and opened the door and then spoke to Tommy. "I want you and Marcus to go out there and bring lots of snow into the bus."

Tommy looked at me questioningly, but he obeyed. Loaded up with snow, he and Marcus climbed back in. I then instructed my passengers in the fine art of making high-quality snowballs. I made one for myself.

Then I slowly pulled the bus around the corner and up the street. We spotted the kid who had pelted us ahead on the sidewalk. Slowly the windows on the bus went down, and I opened my own.

When we were next to the kid, I heaved my snowball. Simultaneously, snowballs began to fly out of the bus as our tormentor stared open-mouthed. It may have been Tommy's snowball that made the biggest impact. Cheers filled Bus 11-A.

I immediately felt guilty about what I had put them up to. But we were Bus 11-A, and I was tired of others making fun of my friends. Yes, mentally handicapped friends like Tommy. Maybe I did feel sorry for him. He was good-looking and robust, and it was sad that he didn't have a strong mentality. Still, my feelings for him went deeper than pity. Our friendship transcended trivial conversations about his five girlfriends.

As the cheering and laughter died, Tommy seemed to sense my mood.

"You OK, Randy?"

"Yeah. Is everything all right with you, Tommy?"

"It OK," he replied. "I—mmm—just thinkin' about something."

"What's going on inside that head of yours?" I probed.

"Oh, I just thinkin'. About—mmm—you," he said. "You know what we like—mmm—most about you, Randy?"

I wondered what aspect of my personality had attracted them. The upcoming party, perhaps? The way I sounded so official when I talked on the two-way radio?

"Go ahead, tell me," I said.

"Randy, what—mmm—we like most about—mmm—you, is that you're just like one of us!"

His comment caught me off-guard. Just like one of *them*? And then suddenly, what a few months earlier would've been an insult, now struck me as the highest of compliments and came from a deep place in my friend's heart.

"Um, well, hey, thanks, Tommy."

I couldn't say more just then, but Tommy understood.

*   *   *

By now I've lost track of my former passengers, but I cherish their memory and the privilege of hauling them around. The irony of someone with his own set of mental disorders transporting a busload of mentally challenged individuals is beyond ironic, almost, well, crazy. But then, maybe we all have "issues"; perhaps some are just more evident than others. A couple of my short-bus homies couldn't have hidden their severe symptoms any more than I could've transformed Bus 11-A into a magic carpet. My challenges, on the other hand, don't tend to manifest themselves in a way that others readily perceive as my being a little off-center. Tommy didn't know it, but in some ways, I'm a lot more like one of them than he realized. No, I no longer harbor some kind of irrational fear that being around mentally handicapped persons will suck me into some kind of mental illness vortex from which there is no escape. But I do have other challenges, and just like my passengers, I'm doing the best I can to work with them.

One afternoon while driving Bus 11-A, I began experiencing an odd chest sensation. Every once in a while, my heart seemed to miss a beat.

"Bus 11-A to base." Uncertain of what was happening to me physically, I figured that I had better not put my riders at risk, so I radioed in my situation.

"OK, pull over, and we'll send out a relief driver," came the response from the dispatcher. Some twenty minutes later, I relinquished my driver's seat to my replacement. I was given a ride home, hopeful that this would not be a recurring event.

But my hopes were not realized. Several nights later, I experienced the same erratic heartbeat. Sharon, a nurse friend who happened to be living with our family at the time, drove me to the local emergency room. There, as had happened so often in the past, the doctor told me there was nothing wrong with me. He said that such incidents involve what are called "palpitations" and that typically, they are not dangerous. Later, I would discover that "heart palpitations are one of the most common causes of the fluttering sensation people refer to as the heart skipping a beat. This can feel like you have skipped beats or your heart stopped beating for a few moments. It can also feel as though you are suddenly very aware of your own heartbeat because it is racing or there is a pounding sensation in the neck, throat or chest. This can be caused by diet pills, excessive exercise, fever, high use of illegal drugs, caffeine or nicotine or anxiety and panic attacks. In more severe cases this could be a sign that you have an abnormal heart valve, overactive thyroid, low oxygen levels or heart disease."[1]

The general medical consensus is that my particular type of irregular heartbeat is not terribly dangerous. Perhaps to help assuage my fears, that night the emergency room doctor handed me a prescription for Inderal®, a drug used to help address this type of problem. I don't recall ever taking any of the pills, because the palpitations weren't occurring that often. Their onset was not yet predictable, so I chose to simply live with them rather than constantly take a medication. Behind the headlines of this choice, of course, was my fear that somehow introducing a foreign substance into my bloodstream might somehow cause me to lose control of some aspect of my personhood. This fear was both illogical and ill-defined, yet lingered as a reality in the recesses of my psyche.

Over the years, it has become clear that my heart palpitations, which I still experience occasionally decades later, are triggered by stress and anxiety. For example, one evening I received a phone call informing me that my father had suffered a heart attack, and there was some question as to whether or not he would survive until the next morning. The stress of that situation left my heart beating irregularly all night long. (My dad would go on to survive many physical challenges, including another heart attack, being struck by a car while crossing the street, and a stroke.) In my case, rather than caffeine or a faulty thyroid gland, the likely culprit at the root of my heart arrhythmias is the chemical cortisol, one of the three major stress hormones (adrenaline and norepinephrine are the other two) associated with the sympathetic nervous system. In other words, the same "fight or flight" response that leads to a panic attack can sometimes produce irregular heartbeats under other circumstances.

Perhaps someday various symptoms such as mine will be easily diagnosed as part of a highly specific biochemical and physiological package. Since the time I began dealing with my various challenges, the mid-1960s, huge progress has been made, with a variety of diagnostic and treatment options becoming increasingly available. Yet ironically, the same process that leads to great discoveries and hopeful solutions often exposes other previously unknown causal elements. The complexities involved can seem overwhelming. Still, relief is in more abundant supply than ever before, at least in developed societies.

Wouldn't it be great if a person could just stop thinking anxious thoughts? Toward that end, some therapists utilize "thought stopping"—a protocol unique to cognitive-behavioral therapists—and it's not always viewed positively in the psychotherapeutic community. Some non-cognitive-behavioral therapists believe that thought stopping actually perpetuates avoidance and can make things worse over time, leading to something called "rebounding." In a post on PsychologyToday.com, Robert L. Leahy, Ph.D., writes, "'Thought-stopping' is a now discarded behavioral technique that involves getting rid of negative or unwanted thoughts by suppressing them. Thus, whenever you have the worry that you will lose all your money in the stock market, you are encouraged to force yourself to stop having these thoughts by snapping a rubber band on your wrist (to distract you) or just yelling to yourself, 'Stop.' This is supposed to reduce your worries. Unfortunately, thought stopping not only does not work, it actually leads to 'thought-rebounding' and makes things worse in the long term." Leahy explains what *really* happens: "Thought-rebounding occurs because you cannot eliminate thoughts that are in your mind—you cannot erase your memory. Not only is it impossible to erase your memory, but by actively engaging in suppressing a thought you must pay attention to the thought—you must actually look for the thought that you are trying to suppress!"[2]

Thought-stopping also doesn't challenge the emotions from the amygdala that override our thoughts. That's why it's especially important to ask the question, "So what?" Ultimately, the fearful person needs to understand what's actually involved in the worst-case scenario or feared situation that's being avoided. This is another reason to work with a therapist. A good therapist is one who understands anxiety disorders and seeks to work alongside medication in unpacking emotions and feared scenarios. (We'll look at "thought-*challenging*" in chapter 10.)

Telling an anxious person to just stop thinking about the problem is insensitive and stems from a lack of psychological understanding. Better to listen and strive to *hear* the sufferer's pain. Well-intentioned but uninformed advice can bring more harm than healing. Please don't be that person.

NINE

MUHAMMAD ALI'S WIFE AND THE MATTRESS

With marriage just one week away, great responsibilities lay just ahead, both personally and financially. So I did what seemed most logical at the time: I quit my job.

As rewarding as driving Bus 11-A had proved to be, I had more creative ideas in mind for becoming financially secure.

"Your mind is in a constant state of 'creative ferment'," one therapist opined. As it turns out, researchers have learned that people with anxiety challenges such as obsessive-compulsive disorder and panic often have a proclivity toward creativity—and higher-than-average intelligence.

Intelligent would not be the first word that came to anyone's mind upon learning that I had just quit my job. But during my first years dabbling in college, I'd worked at a local florist shop and greenhouse. Something about the beauty and orderliness of endless rows of foliage had caught my fancy. But after trying my hand at a small greenhouse venture that catered to supermarkets and chain stores, I eventually came to see that I needed a product with much longer shelf life. Cacti were the logical solution.

I designed an entire line of small wooden planters that contained a variety of cacti in them. They sold well but not well enough to keep the bill collectors at bay. A year into both cacti and marriage, and I knew something had to change if we were to avoid a close encounter with small-claims court and the IRS.

During this same period, I'd begun working with the teen group at our local church. I seemed to have a knack for connecting meaningful spiritual concepts with youths' everyday experience. Could it be possible that something along these lines, rather than becoming a cactus king, was my real destiny?

"Yeah, I guess I really do enjoy writing skits, leading the youth group, and doing things like that for teens," I admitted to Diana one evening.

"Maybe you should call Geof," she suggested.

Geof had been my youth group leader, and I'd also lived with him and his wife, Lynda, in South Carolina for a month during one of my various young-adult solo expeditions. Geof was now a pastor in southern California.

"OK, I'm going to do that right now," I told Diana.

Geof told me what being a real-life youth pastor would be like and the education it would require. I hung up with lots of information, but I was still uncertain about the future.

The next evening, I was on my knees praying, asking for heavenly guidance regarding the next steps to take in my life, when the phone rang. I cut short my spiritual enterprise and answered the call. I was surprised to hear God on the other end of the line. Well, actually, it was Geof, but his voice seemed to carry a distinct otherworldly tone.

"You know, Randy, we have this program out here

called 'Summer Youth Assistant.' If you're interested, you could come out here and be my assistant for the summer and test the youth ministry waters."

I had come to believe that God answers prayer, but within sixty seconds? True, I'd spoken with Geof the previous evening, but somehow this seemed more than a mere earthly arrangement.

I hung up the phone, and Diana and I discussed the opportunity. It seemed to both of us that this could be more than happenstance. Still, she was working for the university in its Placement Services office and shouldered significant responsibilities. "You may have to go out there alone," she gently told me. "I'm not sure it's a good idea for me to take the entire summer off."

My heart sank. We'd been married for less than two years—no way did I want to leave my wife for an entire summer! *What kind of marriage would that be?* I thought.

But there was another reason for my apprehension. By this time in my life I'd become somewhat of a master at hiding my struggle with anxiety. Teens and others viewed me as laid-back and cool—the very antithesis of the turmoil within. I'd even kept the matter at bay with Diana, who knew little of my growing dysfunction.

I look back with no small degree of shame at the arguments I presented to Diana against separating for the summer. But I knew there was no way I could go west alone. Panic and phobic behavior already held a strong grip on me, and Diana had become my "safe person."

I had become agoraphobic.

In the original language (Greek), the term *agoraphobia*

technically means "fear of the marketplace." The *agora* was the public shopping area, a place bustling with commercial activity. *Phobia,* of course, is an extreme fear of something or someone. Some real but lesser-known phobias include:

- arachibutyrophobia (fear of peanut butter sticking to the roof of one's mouth)

- bolshephobia (fear of meeting or hearing about Bolsheviks)

- cainophobia (fear of anything new)

- deipnophobia (fear of dining in public)

- phobophobia (you guessed it—fear of having a phobia)

- scriptophobia (fear of writing in public)

- venustraphobia (fear of beautiful women)[1]

Before my own rendezvous with a phobia, I might have questioned whether these fears actually existed. Today, I have no doubt. Phobias can be very real—and very crippling. Few understand just how draining these behaviors can be on loved ones and others surrounding those afflicted with these irrational fears.

The preceding definition of agoraphobia is not the best one, in my opinion. While it can be uncomfortable for agoraphobics to be in public places, often that is not the core fear. For most agoraphobic persons, it is the *fear of experiencing panic or a loss of control* that keeps the phobia alive. In other words, it's a fear of fear that's the real issue. (I do not know whether Franklin D. Roosevelt, who famously said, "The only thing we have to fear is fear itself," was agoraphobic. There is some indication that he did suffer from triskadekaphobia—fear of the number 13.)

The definition of agoraphobia that I suggest certainly applied in my case. My most intense experience with panic had taken place on a Chicago freeway, and it resulted in this faulty syllogism:

Panic attacks exist.
I had a panic attack while traveling alone.
Traveling alone causes panic attacks.

No, traveling alone did *not* lie at the root of my panic attacks, but the cause and effect was too strong in my subconscious mind to see beyond. With this twisted logic firmly in place, I began attaching myself to safety zones: people and places that kept me emotionally rooted in the predictable known rather than the fearful unknown. Diana was not the only "safe" person in my life, but since she was the most convenient, she unwittingly assumed the primary role.

Little of this was on my conscious radar. At age 24, I had a vague sense that something wasn't normal, but it was all very hazy—and unnerving. I couldn't identify, let alone articulate, a core issue or causation for my growing discomfort. At the time, I'd never heard anyone talk about the kinds of symptoms I was experiencing. Surely, I was the only person in the entire world enduring such manifestations. I could not bear the thought that maybe, just maybe, I was at least a little . . . crazy, so I continued busying myself to avoid considering such a possibility.

A California expedition was a perfect distraction. Diana had finally agreed to stick with me for the summer. My exploration of youth ministry as a possible profession had begun.

Our housing in the Riverside, California, area was a small bungalow—a cottage, really—tucked behind a larger house in a suburban area. Any hope of relief from the heat was provided by what was called a "swamp cooler"—some kind of faux air conditioner whose operational principles I still do not understand. I can tell you that in the matter of coolness, this particular unit was about as effective as a tray of ice cubes set out on the kitchen table.

To my great joy, the church's youth group quickly accepted me, either because I was a Midwestern curiosity or because they actually liked me. Either way, things went well. That is, until Diana decided she wanted to go spend some time with her aunt in San Diego, which would leave me home alone.

True, I hadn't needed Diana to accompany me as I drove around the relatively small area in which I carried out my various summer responsibilities. But San Diego would place her a hundred miles away. Being that far from my chosen "safe person" made me sweat. Still, I wasn't about to tell Diana any of this, so I kissed her good-bye and wished her a good time. She headed south on I-15, clueless about my already-rising anxiety level.

I stayed up late that night praying, listening to the radio, and forcing myself to mentally engage in anything other than the fact that I was in a relatively unfamiliar community without my wife. It was the first time we'd been apart since becoming husband and wife, and I didn't like the feeling—for the strangest of reasons. How could a grown man be experiencing the separation anxiety of a 2-year-old?

Somehow, I managed to perform enough mind tricks to get through this and similar incidents. The summer ended on a high note, as it became clear that the church's youth group had truly bonded with me. Convinced that a clear career path lay ahead, Diana and I returned to Michigan, where I enrolled in the university's undergraduate theological program. Along with learning biblical Greek and studying Christian ethics, I would soon be elected president of the university's ministerial club. Working with a local youth group, Diana and I found deep satisfaction in helping them to perform various Christian dramas. The spectrum of busyness helped to keep my growing anxiety disorder buried enough to make progress on my academic and career pursuits.

A few weeks after our return from California, Geof, who'd been the full-time youth pastor at the church where I'd done my summer stint, called to let me know that he'd accepted a similar position in San Diego. A few days later, our phone rang.

"Randy, this is Pastor Cal calling." I recognized the resonant voice of Geof's former senior pastor. Soon, it became clear that he was probing to see if I might be a good fit to replace Geof as youth pastor at the church where we'd served that summer. "The teens seemed to really like you," he affirmed.

Something else soon became clear: Pastor Cal thought I was already in seminary, not still in college. When the reality sank in that it would be at least another year before I completed the required coursework to become a serious candidate for the position, the conversation ended.

[*131*]

Still, my life seemed on a positive trajectory. I was making good commissions working part-time at a local furniture store, surviving Greek classes, and establishing a name for myself around campus. Life was good—so long as I didn't have to drive very far alone.

In California, a church staff member had taught me how to tune pianos. I figured it could help provide a little extra income during the college years, belated as they were for me.

By this time, the "old school" method of tuning pianos had a fresh competitor: electronic tuners had just made their way onto the market. My chosen tuner was the Peterson 420 Stroboscopic Tuner. Since the Internet was still somewhat an academic and military secret at the time, the closest location to purchase the tuner was some distance away, near South Bend, Indiana. The night before, I pushed out of my mind the fact that I'd be well out of range of any safe person or safe place. Add to that the fact that I really wanted to get my hands on that tuning device, and the following morning found me setting sail alone for the tuner dealer. As I passed Notre Dame University, my discomfort was still minimal. That changed a few miles later, when my breathing began growing shallow. Soon, the familiar clouds of panic began gathering, full force.

I was just a couple of miles from my destination when I figured I had to do something. Pulling into a gas station, I shakily walked inside and asked for directions to the music dealership. As the person spoke, my panic symptoms subsided; apparently, the conversation was just enough to switch my gaze from an inward focus to my current surroundings. I continued on my journey, purchased the tuner, and drove back home, though above the speed limit.

Later, I thought about what had happened. On that day, for the first time, I silently admitted that something really was wrong with me. Had the very thing I feared most—a mental illness—become a reality?

College classes went well that school year, and Pastor Geof offered me another summer opportunity as his youth ministry assistant. He was now youth pastor at a church in National City, near San Diego. We'd be staying with Diana's aunt in Poway, California, about twenty-five miles north of where I'd be working.

One morning as I headed down I-15 toward San Diego, I took conscious notice of something I'd been doing for a while now. As I passed each off-ramp, I asked myself a question: *Do I know anyone who lives around here?* Later, I realized that I was doing an SPS—a "safe person search." That is, I was ensuring that if I had a panic attack, I could get to a familiar person before something awful occurred, whatever that might be. Surely, the safe person wouldn't let anything bad happen! Exactly what would happen should I come to an exit where nobody resided whom I knew was anybody's guess. Usually, I convinced myself that *someone* would be available in an emergency.

The summer passed, and we returned to Michigan, where I'd face another year of Greek and other classroom miseries. As part of the theology department's protocol, we were encouraged to send résumés across the country, partially in hopes that the department could boast a satisfactory placement ratio. About halfway through the year, our denomination's representatives from the state of Michigan interviewed Diana and I as a prospective pastoral couple.

(I cannot speak for other denominations, but in our denomination the "brethren"—that is, the hiring committee—somewhat assumed that a candidate's wife would come free as part of the pastoral package. I suspect that many a lackluster pastor has been hired because his wife was a social animal and could play a mean piano.)

I'd be fibbing if I told you that I thought the recruiting team was more impressed with me than they were with Diana. The end result was that the hiring committee voted to financially sponsor the next leg of my academic journey: seminary. This meant that rather than venturing forth as an assistant pastor upon graduation, I would simply move from one building on campus to another, where I would begin work on my Master of Divinity degree. This came as no small relief, since it meant I'd be able to continue going about my life within a few-miles radius. My fear of driving alone now seemed to be escalating by the day. Thankfully, my furniture-selling job was just a mile away, and pretty much everything else I needed wasn't much farther in distance, such as my psychotherapist. Dr. Baker continued exploring with me the challenges at hand. Counting things and clicking my teeth came and went, but the panic and my ever-increasing driving anxieties were taking a toll on me—including physically.

My weekday schedule typically found me attending classes in the morning and selling home furnishings and floor covering in the late afternoon and evening. As an introvert, it's strange how much I enjoyed my sales role. I was good at it, not to mention that it was a pleasant departure from the brain drain taking place at the hands of my seminary professors.

By this time, as a result of combined stress, a well-intentioned effort to adopt an ultra-healthy diet, and regular exercise, my already lean body had taken an even further nosedive: I weighed in at 116 pounds while standing roughly 5'9" tall. When Diana and I attended a health seminar at the university, the sponsors were alarmed to find my body fat ratio to be an unhealthy 3 percent.

One evening at the furniture store, an acquaintance I'd not seen for some time walked through the establishment's front doors. "Hello, Mrs. Kingsley," I greeted in my most charming sales voice.

Her response was unexpected. Looking at me with a mildly shocked expression, she blurted out, "You sure are skinny! Have you been sick?"

Several retorts came to mind, including, "Well, you certainly are looking huge these days, Mrs. Kingsley. Have you been hitting the chocolate eclairs again?" But this is hardly the stuff of which budding pastors are made, so I simply switched the conversation and led her toward the dinette sets.

"May I help you find something?" I greeted the two customers as they entered the furniture store. An African-American woman, probably in her early 40s, entered the store with an older woman. It quickly became clear that this was a mother-daughter duo out on a furniture bargain-hunting mission. They were especially interested in a sectional sofa, and we dickered until the price seemed right to all parties. At the sales desk, my eyes opened wide when I noticed there were two names on the check, one of which was Muhammad Ali. I didn't say much about it, because a few puzzle pieces were beginning to fall into place.

Several years earlier, the world-champion boxer had purchased an unusual property adjacent to our town's little university. The home was built in the early 1900s by Al Capagna, an associate of Al Capone. Rumors of escape tunnels leading to the nearby St. Joseph River and bullet holes in the home's walls had circulated for decades, few of which had ever been proved true. But it was a fact that Muhammad Ali had now taken up residence in the house—I'd even seen his Rolls Royce in town. He'd converted one of the farm's barns into a training center, where I'd once watched him train for his eventual world heavyweight contest with Joe Frazier. Now it seemed that he was betrothed to Yolanda, whom I came to know as "Lonnie." She was updating some of the home's living spaces and had decided to "shop local." Over time, along with the sectional sofa, I sold several other items to the Alis, including carpeting and vinyl flooring for their kitchen. (One day I called their house, and her husband answered. It probably took him a while to figure out how I managed to get his home phone number.)

One day Lonnie and her mother came in to look at mattresses. Mother would be staying in an upstairs bedroom, and she had some memorable comments regarding the Champ's former wife's taste in color. But they would have to go elsewhere for wall paint. I could help her get a good night's sleep, however.

"For this particular bedroom, we'll need a double-sized mattress," Lonnie informed me. "And we need it right away."

Problem. The store's inventory was low, and we had

only one double-sized mattress set in stock. Beyond that, however, was another problem: my ultra-sensitive conscience. This particular mattress set had been previously sold and used—for exactly one night. Apparently, it lacked some element the purchaser had been looking for, and it had been picked up for resale. Technically, it was now a used mattress, something a family whose wheels were a Rolls Royce would likely not be interested in purchasing.

The inward battle raged. *But it was used for just one night, for pity's sake!* I reasoned. *Surely it still constitutes a* new *mattress!* On the other hand, the word *used* was hard to escape in the immediate context. Would I suffer eternal consequences if I didn't tell my valued customer about this little wrinkle? Or was I making a mountain of mental anguish out of an ethical molehill?

Finally, I decided that if *I* were to get a good night's sleep, I'd have to 'fess up, hopefully, without losing the sale. After showing the mattress, now rewrapped in plastic, to my customers, we sealed the deal.[2] At the sales counter, as Lonnie pulled out the now-familiar checkbook yet another time, I casually mentioned that the mattress had been tried for one night by a customer.

"You mean this is a *used* mattress!" her mother said incredulously. My ploy was unraveling before my very eyes! I waited for the other shoe to drop; that is, Lonnie's checkbook. But it didn't happen. Instead, she simply said, "Oh, that's OK," and went on writing the check.

Lonnie later told me that beneath her husband's bluster resided a "heart of gold." Apparently, some of it had rubbed off on her.

Had the whole exercise even been necessary? I still

don't know. All I know is that I had exhibited yet another trait common to many anxiety sufferers, especially those with a bent toward spirituality: ensuring that not even one grain of unconscionable behavior be entertained. Every molecule of the conscience must be in perfect order, lest something really bad happen.

At the end of the day, I celebrated the sale but lamented the insufferable reality of my insatiable need to be certain that I hadn't committed a grievous sin.

A sensitive nature is both a blessing and a curse. Among the blessings can be high ethical and moral standards, exceptional creativity, a natural inclination to think before speaking, and a strong sense of empathy. Often, people whose consciences are ultrasensitive are also more reactive to physical stimuli. The bottom line is that, as author Deborah Ward points out:

"Because highly sensitive people absorb so much stimulation from their environment, we are more susceptible to . . . feelings of anxiety. A recent study showed that people with a more sensitive 'startle' reflex, that is, highly sensitive people, are more susceptible to anxiety disorders because we have different genes than others, making it harder for us to deal with emotional arousal."[3]

Yeah, that's me.

Life would be a whole lot easier for people like me if we'd been served up a different personality at birth. But our genetic code is what it is. Perhaps the day will come when DNA strands will be swapped out with "after-market" replacements more to our liking. Until then, we can choose to embrace the benefits and creatively cope with the challenges.

TEN

"IT" HAS A NAME

My seminary dean got straight to the point: "We need to get you out of here." I was in my second year of the two-year graduate-level seminary program, and I was just flat burned out from reading such scintillating volumes as *Lectures on Systematic Theology* and *The Sabbath in Scripture and History*. My seminary dean knew full well that I was not wired to survive such fare for long, and now he was bending over backward to provide academic credit for some previous writing that I'd done on the subject of youth ministry. The German theologian-turned-seminary dean was known as a rigorous scholar with very high academic standards. He graciously lowered them on my behalf, and his effort to help boot me out of Seminary Hall and into the real world as quickly as possible was deeply appreciated.[1]

By this time, agoraphobia had a relentless grip on me. We'd moved from our tiny upstairs apartment into a small, older house owned by the university. (When we had a seminary professor over one evening, he looked around the interior of our home and stated, "Yes, I remember when these houses were the cream of the crop." That was before they were all razed; today there is a vast expanse of grass where this section of student housing once existed.) No passersby could have known the level of psychological trauma taking place inside the student shack situated at 17 Maple Street.

The Master of Divinity coursework included being assigned to help out at a local church. I was slated to assist a church in Eau Claire, Michigan, about six miles from the university campus. To my great delight, the church had an attached school, and attached to the school was a dilapidated greenhouse. *This is going to be perfect!* I thought. With my background in greenhouse work, I quickly got permission from the school administration to rehab the little structure. My goal was to have the eighth-graders grow tomato plants, the proceeds of which would benefit their various class endeavors.

Toward the beginning, driving the six miles to the school was challenging but not impossible. Many were the times when I came close to giving in to the panic symptoms that swept over me. But over the course of several weeks, I found that I could make the drive relatively smoothly—during daylight hours. But an increased sense of foreboding crept up whenever the sun went down. I soon discovered that, at night, I could not drive alone a distance of more than *three blocks* without experiencing severe panic.

The tomato-plant venture was a grand success, at least in terms of building relationships with the eighth-graders. The class didn't get rich from it, but the greenhouse was in good shape and, hopefully, the kids had learned a little bit about growing things.

The good news was that tomatoes don't need any care at night. The "bad" news was that the eighth-graders had invited me to deliver their commencement address at year's end, an evening event. *Here we go again,* I thought.

Diana might have come along anyway, but as we drove to the graduation ceremony, I felt like a total failure as a human being, stripped of his masculinity. As usual, shame was the order of the day, and in this case, the night as well.

In case the reader is still foggy on what exactly constitutes agoraphobia, "Typically, people with agoraphobia restrict themselves to a 'zone of safety' that may include only the home or the immediate neighborhood. Any movement beyond the edges of this zone creates mounting anxiety. Even when they restrict themselves to 'safe' situations, most people with agoraphobia continue to have panic attacks at least a few times a month."[2]

What the description didn't mention is that the more creative (dysfunctional?) among us take our "safety zone" along with us, which in my case was my wife. Although I was not completely anxiety-free in her presence, I could drive long distances whenever she came along for the ride, daytime or nighttime. That's how I'd twice been able to get to California and back. Somehow, I'd convinced my subconscious that, in the event of a panic episode, everything would be OK so long as my "safe person" was close at hand.

By this time, I'd learned that panic attacks were usually short-lived, and they really presented no danger—horrible to endure, but nothing to worry about. Had I been able to convince myself of this truth, perhaps the entire arc of my life would have been different.

Earlier, I mentioned the "fight or flight" nature of panic. One author provides this more in-depth description of the chemical surge that accompanies panic:

> All that stuff [fight-or-flight reactions] happens with animals, too, when they're being chased. If you're an antelope, and you're being chased by a pack of bloodthirsty hyenas, you're having this same thing happen, and maybe you're thinking, *This is awesome; my whole antelope body is making me run faster than I ever thought I could. I love the way I'm equipped with this very cool fight-or-flight system.*
>
> Thing is, for the antelope, the whole thing is over pretty quick. I mean, he either gets away from the hyenas or he doesn't. In either case, the whole physiological reaction is short-lived. Just a quick blast, really. That's what fight or flight is for.
>
> Zebras have very real threats but don't get ulcers because that stress-response episode is here and gone in seconds. But we humans—we highly intelligent, top-of-the-food-chain, we-can-put-one-of-us-on-the-moon humans, *invent* things to make us feel threatened. . . . We are capable of imagining threats and staying in a kind of constant, low-grade fight-or-flight mode. We're capable of feeling threatened all the time, by things that haven't even happened and may not ever happen.[3]

So the biochemistry of panic normally doesn't last very

long. But forcing myself to embrace this simple truth and get on with my life was not a mind-set I could muster. Could I have spared decades of mental distress by doing so? Knowing what I do now, while it looks good in theory, I have my doubts that simply grinding it out would've made the difference.

Some therapists would disagree. A particular stripe of therapy called rational emotive behavior therapy (REBT) has helped some people to recover from anxiety disorders. The idea behind this treatment, a form of cognitive-behavioral therapy (CBT), is to challenge and replace one's thinking about a situation or circumstances. (This is different from "thought-stopping.") In the case of agoraphobia, a therapist might challenge the sufferer's belief about something horrible happening:

> *Client:* If I drive at night alone, I might have a panic attack and faint.
> *Therapist:* Have you ever fainted during or after a panic attack?
> *Client:* No.
> *Therapist*: What is the worst that could happen?
> *Client:* I suppose the worst that could happen is that I would pull over to the side of the road and let the panic attack subside. I could breathe into the paper bag I keep in my glovebox to help the symptoms pass more quickly.

Thought challenges sometimes go much deeper, probing for underlying thoughts that might be fostering anxiety. For example, a therapist trained in this area might wish to help the client develop a greater awareness of their fears and to have a corrective emotional experience about it. Ultimately, the goal is to have the client accept the situation rather than fear it.

You get the idea. Yes, some situations can be tough to think about. But it's worth keeping in mind that discomfort does not equal impending death. I like what Duke Ellington said: "There are two kinds of worries—those you can do something about and those you can't. Don't spend any time on the latter." I would only add that if you *do* spend time worrying about what *might* happen, make sure you already have the right response in mind. That means you've done something about it!

I see great value in these and related therapies as part of an overall treatment plan, a fact borne out in many clinical studies. But just as with medication alone, I caution the reader about automatically relying on cognitive therapies alone. Anxiety disorders are complex, but with the right professionals in the picture bringing the proper protocols into play, great hope and change is likely soon to happen for the sufferer.-

At this point, I still didn't even know exactly what was wrong with me. And if I didn't know what was wrong, how could I figure out what needed fixing?

In my never-ending quest to keep anxiety at bay, I continued jogging—seven days a week. Still not eating properly, I probably should've died, or at the very least collapsed from a combination of malnutrition and emotional exhaustion. But the body can sometimes endure immense mistreatment.

One evening, I closed my Hebrew primer and decided to go for a run. Soon, I was doing laps around the block, the muggy summer Michigan air adding to my sweat. I usually didn't have a listening device with me, but for some reason this time I'd hooked an FM radio onto my belt. As I jogged around and around the block, I tuned in to a Christian radio station. The program *Focus on the Family* was airing, and Dr. James Dobson was interviewing a woman whose name was unfamiliar to me. But I slowed my pace as she began describing symptoms of a certain disorder that was apparently the topic of the show.

"Victims often think they're going crazy. Their heart beats rapidly, their hands grow tingly, and they begin to hyperventilate," she explained. "After this happens enough times, they begin avoiding places where the attacks have occurred, such as on highways."

W-wait a minute! I thought. *She sounds like she's talking about* me*!* I turned up the volume.

"Do the symptoms ever get worse?" asked Dr. Dobson.

"What happens is that these people often develop what's called 'agoraphobia.' This is a disorder that finds people increasingly confined to what they consider a 'safety zone.' In the worst-case scenario, victims can become totally housebound."

I was stunned. Before that evening, I was absolutely convinced that I was the only person in the world experiencing these symptoms. I knew something was wrong, but I never would have believed that not only were others going through this ordeal, but that it actually had a name! How ironic that a euphoria should sweep over me upon learning that I had a certified mental disorder!

The woman on the radio was with an organization called TERRAP, which stood for "territorial apprehensiveness." Their program was designed to help people like me overcome the fear of leaving our safety zone. I sent away for their brochure and learned that the program included a variety of body relaxation exercises, thought-change techniques, and "in vivo desensitization." This is where a person takes small steps toward achieving the goal of being able to overcome a particular fear or phobia. In my case, it would mean driving a little farther each day over a period of weeks or months until, supposedly, I'd be able to resume normal travel.

I also learned that the program was unaffordable to someone attending seminary and that it was not offered anywhere close to the state of Michigan. Still, it was a thread of hope onto which I desperately clung.

In Australia, Dr. Claire Weekes was raising consciousness about agoraphobia. Dr. Weekes is considered by some to be a pioneer in the area of anxiety treatment, her preferred method being cognitive therapy. As one who has suffered from agoraphobia, I can attest to the fact that she had a firm grasp of the condition's manifestations:

> The sufferer from agoraphobia does not really think some particular place holds a special danger for him and that something there will harm him. He is afraid of how he will *react* in a certain situation. He has become so sensitively aware of what happens within himself at the slightest stress—of how he panics, feels weak and giddy, and so on—that he lives in fear that these feelings will arise in places where he thinks he will be unable to cope with them and where he may consequently make a fool of himself in front of others. So the housewife clings to her home and the executive to his own hometown. They cling to

their safety zone. This is why the nervous person sits at the back of the school meeting, on the aisle at the cinema, near the door in the restaurant—so that he can slip out quickly and unnoticed if he feels one of his turns coming. He specially dreads being in an airplane, a train, any vehicle he cannot stop and leave at will.[4]

Bingo.

But here's where there *may* be a gap between Weekes' understanding of agoraphobia and more recent research. Weekes was confident that most agoraphobia could be overcome by proper thinking and real-life (in vivo) practice. This involved applying the four following principles upon the arrival of a panic episode:

▸ Face; do not run away.

▸ Accept; do not fight.

▸ Float past; do not arrest and listen in.

▸ Let time pass; do not be impatient with time.[5]

According to Weekes, "The surest path to permanent recovery is to know how to face, and try to accept, fear and not to placate it with subterfuge."[6]

Weekes chalks up panic and agoraphobia to "sensitized nerves." According to her, "The symptoms of much nervous illness are no more than the symptoms of stress exaggerated by severe sensitization."[7] Later, she adds, "Sensitized nerves heal as natural as a broken leg, but it takes time."[8]

So do I think Weekes is right in asserting that panic can be controlled—and eventually eliminated—essentially by willpower alone? While not discounting the value of Weekes' contributions, in today's medical environment, with a vast array of modern diagnostic tools, the "sensitized nerves" theory may paint only a partial picture, an example of which follows shortly.

In the end, Weekes' approach does not seem to promise ultimate cure in its purest form but rather, acceptance of the symptoms, which may become less and less frightening over time. True acceptance means even welcoming panic so you can practice coping with it the way I have advised until it no longer frightens.[9]

Ultimately, she defines recovery in this way: "Recovery is the final establishment of the right attitude of mind."[10]

As I've noted, willpower seems paramount in Weekes' approach to dealing with agoraphobia, something that can be in short supply after years of suffering panic attacks and its attendant downward spiral.

Still, I think there is more truth than error in her understanding of the dysfunction. Virtually everything she has written on the subject rings true, at least in the way agoraphobia works. I suspect that many people who are able to face their fear and panic, and the "second fear" Weekes also speaks about (the fear that escalates by focusing on the symptoms themselves), might indeed overcome many of their agoraphobic symptoms. She is also correct in her assessment regarding the "fear-adrenaline-fear" cycle, which leads to the irrefutable conclusion that "there is a limit to the intensity of a spasm of panic even a sensitized body can produce."[11] As a result, it would be foolish to undervalue Weekes' contributions to the understanding of agoraphobia. But as I earlier implied, modern science has added vital information to the treatment of agoraphobia that even Weekes herself would most assuredly embrace. While she did not reject a patient's initial need for medication, it seems that she saw it only as a temporary measure to be employed until the person could muster enough courage to accept the distress brought on by a "sensitized" nervous system.

Again, I speak from experience and not medical training. But current modern diagnostic methods and research seem to point toward a more complex mind-body relationship than Weekes may have understood during her time. For example, one study reported that

> Stewart et al. (1988) used single photon emission computed tomography (SPECT) to investigate the cerebral blood flow in panic disorder patients and healthy controls comparing the baseline levels with data gathered after infusion of saline and sodium lactate. They measured regional blood flow in frontal, temporal, parietal occipital and superior temporal areas of cortex, total blood flow in each hemisphere as well as whole brain blood flow. The PD patients who panicked with sodium lactate infusion had significantly greater increased blood flow in the right occipital region. However, whereas the hemispheric and whole brain blood flow of healthy subjects and patients who did not panic were significantly increased after lactate infusion in comparison to baseline and saline infusion, only small increases or even decreases were observed in the panicking patients. . . . There is now evidence suggesting that the permeability of the blood-brain

barrier might be implicated in the development and treatment of panic disorder.[12]

This is just one example of the breathtaking discoveries being made so often in the area of mental health. I am confident that Claire Weekes would be thrilled with this progress, as well.

Scientific research has revealed much about the physiological component of other anxiety-related disorders besides agoraphobia. In *The Highly-Sensitive Person,* Dr. Elanie Aron writes:

> When under stress, [sensitive childrens'] pupils dilate sooner, and their vocal cords are more tense, making their voice change to a higher pitch. (Many HSPs [highly-sensitive persons] are relieved to know why their voice can become so strange sounding when they are aroused.)

> The body fluids (blood, urine, saliva, of sensitive children show indications of high levels of norepinephrine present in their brains, especially after the children are exposed to various forms of stress in the laboratory. Norephinephrine is associated with arousal; in fact, it is the brain's version of adrenaline. Sensitive children's body fluids also contain more cortisol, both when under stress and when at home. Cortisol is the hormone present when one is in a more or less constant state of arousal or wariness.[13]

Aron goes on:

Other studies have also found that many HSPs have more activity in the right hemisphere of the brain, especially those who stay sensitive from birth into childhood—that is, were clearly born that way.[14]

I include this information not to imply that all sensitive children or adults are prone to develop an anxiety disorder. But I am convinced that it is yet another indication that genetic factors do in fact play a key role in one's propensity to develop problems in the area of anxiety. I score very high on the "highly-sensitive person scale," and Aron's insights reflect my experience.

Obsessive-compulsive disorder, as well, clearly has a strong biological component. In his book about his own struggles with the disorder, author of *The Man Who Couldn't Stop* and an editor at *Nature*, David Adam, points out:

> Hundreds of OCD patients have been MRI scanned over the last decade or so, and had their brains compared to those of normal people, schizophrenics and hoarders. They have been scanned before and after treatment, and while they rest or wrestle with deliberately planted intrusive thoughts. Again and again a consistent picture of OCD emerges—unusual activity in and around a brain region called the basal ganglia.[15]

In other words, there's a lot more going on behind our eyeballs than we realize.

ELEVEN

THE WORST VACATION EVER

Seminary classes went year-round, and Diana would be going on vacation with her family to Minnesota while I continued studying missiology and Old Testament prophets. Secretly, I knew the departure of my wife, the only real "safe person" in my life, would present a severe challenge to my ability to function.

The Saturday night before her departure, my anxiety escalated to a nearly unbearable level. With Diana out of the house for a few minutes, I sank to the floor of our small living room and began rocking back and forth on my knees. *God, please do something—anything—to fix me!* I pleaded. *I can't take it!* Desperately, I dug my fingernails into the carpet and began clawing it like a cat. What was I afraid of? What did I think would happen? As usual, it all had something to do with overwhelming fear and a loss of control. A distant, vague threat that somehow my personhood would implode hung over me. Would I do something so socially unacceptable in public that my entire future would be jeopardized? "What if?" grooves were by now deeply etched in my brain.

I'd read stories of people who, when praying about difficult circumstances, felt a sudden peace "wash over" them. The only thing washing over me was the cold sweat of panic. It seemed clear that God had chosen not to alter time and space to bathe me in serenity.

The next morning, Diana's parents pulled up in front of our little house. As I hauled my wife's suitcase out to the car, my chest felt as though a thousand banshees were trying to beat their way through to freedom. Diana still didn't have a complete grasp of my dysfunction, but after I'd delayed her for thirty minutes, she made a suggestion. "Call Bill and Darcy and ask them to come over here."

Bill was my best friend and seminary buddy, and his wife Darcy was a nurse. What was I going to tell them? "I'm nothing more than a grown-up baby, and I'm crying because my 'mommy' is going away"? But the anxiety was overwhelming. When Bill answered the phone, I mumbled something about needing some help and could they come over right away.

I'm not sure what Diana or I told them when they arrived. I'm sure I laughed and joked with them, which was my preferred way of keeping up appearances. My safe person headed down our front steps and got into her parents' car. Within a few minutes of her departure, panic worked its devilish magic on me, and I moved toward the front door. I intended to get into my car, catch the departing vacationers and, well, I didn't exactly know what. All I knew was that I was disintegrating, and the only thing that would stop it involved being in close proximity to my "safe person."

To her credit, Darcy quickly saw enough to step up, and so did Bill. Blocking the doorway and grasping my shoulders, Bill spoke softly while firmly restraining me. Whatever he said worked in the moment. Slowly, he led me over to the sofa, where my dear friends helped me to breathe slowly and talked me through the worst of the panic.

"Randy, everything is going to be fine," Bill said. I suspect he had no clue about what was actually happening, but in that simple, worn-out phrase he'd dispensed the perfect bromide.

Bill and Darcy stayed for another half hour, talking, distracting me, and otherwise massaging my fear-riddled brain back down to a functional level. I wasn't exactly OK, but the worst seemed to have passed.

The next seven days still claim the prize as the "Longest Week Ever." Without fully divulging the reason behind my invitation, I encouraged some of my youth group to drop by the house that evening. I kept them up longer than they would have otherwise stayed, in an effort to shorten my forthcoming night alone. When one of the girls showed obvious signs of annoyance, I jokingly said, "Well, honestly, I don't do well without my wife." I hoped they'd see it as a funny comment but decide to stay even longer. Instead, the girl blurted out, "What a wimp!"

Yeah, what a wimp.

The next few days were filled with study, work, and an occasional phone call to my therapist. My furniture employer benefited from my dysfunction as—to help keep my mind occupied—I sought out extra tasks such as assembling bookcases. I jogged every day—including a seven-miler—to help lower my anxiety level. Since I remained dangerously slender, I risked serious physical trauma with every step. A consistently irregular heart-beat that week caused me to visit my physician, who expressed concern. "With your weight being what it is, you should probably take it easy on the exercise," he told me. But he wasn't the one trying to survive a week-long stay in hell.

Tears again fill my eyes as I write about these events. Even though it's now so many years later, shades of shame and embarrassment still accompany the memory. Of course, this accomplishes nothing. As Dr. Dean Ornish commented in an interview, "Some of the most toxic emotions are guilt, humiliation, and shame."[1] I could take the witness stand in defense of this statement.

But what *has* changed is my understanding of what actually took place. I wasn't a maladjusted guy with some kind of weird "adult-infant" syndrome. (There is value in an appropriate exploration of that subject, by the way. Dr. Charles Whitfield's now-classic book, *Healing the Child Within*, contains profound insights, and I highly recommend it.) Yes, I had mental disorders, but none had anything to do with "going crazy." I now realize that a very small percentage, if any, of my challenges are rooted in "personal weakness." Certainly, such issues are not the result of spiritual shortcomings, although some well-meaning churchgoers will challenge this assertion. And then there are the quick-fixers, such as the woman who told me after a presentation that ingesting large quantities of cilantro would have cured my panic attacks. Sorry, but I'm not buying it (the theory, that is; I buy cilantro because I happen to like it).

So what, if anything, *could* I buy to fix my problems? A substantial investment in psychotherapy had proved helpful, but it certainly hadn't healed me. After checking into the price of the TERRAP program, I knew it was out of the question for a seminary student. Medication might help to calm me, but I remained resistant to the idea. To my way of thinking, it was a cop-out—a crutch. I could deal with this thing on my own terms, especially now that I knew it had a name.

Foolish thinking.

By now, avoiding travel alone had become a way of life. "Thanks for the invitation to come and preach at your church, but I'm pretty booked right now." "Um, I can't really go measure that house for carpet today. Maybe one of the other guys can cover it." Each day was an endless carousel ride of avoidance and excuses, all because I couldn't function outside my "safety zone" without panic symptoms quickly effervescing. Relying on Diana to accompany me when there was simply no way out of an obligation was demeaning to me and inconvenient to her. But soon things would get better—wouldn't they?

During the height of my battle with anxiety, our family had taken yet another summer vacation to Minnesota, where Diana's extended family has its roots. Anxiety was always on the upswing during travel, even though we'd taken the same route for years. Often during such trips, I'd fight off my torment by engaging my mind in an area that held particular interest: writing. When I was behind the wheel, I'd think of possible story lines, often constructing complete sentences, and occasionally, entire paragraphs in my mind. Then, when Diana slipped behind the wheel, I'd pull out a pen and transfer my mental draft to paper. The first affordable laptop had yet to appear in the marketplace, so I resorted to the ancient craft of writing by hand. Many a tankful of gas was paid for as the result of hours spent fighting off anxious distress in this manner.

Our sleeping accommodations in Minnesota consisted of an old iron-frame bed located in the basement of Diana's grandparents' home. Longtime Swedish farmers in that community, Grandpa and Grandma Blost had now moved into the closest town, where they'd purchased a simple rancher on one of Pine City's side streets. Since the house had no central or window air-conditioning, sleeping in the cool, concrete-floor basement provided some welcome relief from the Minnesota summer heat and humidity.

Unfortunately, it could not relieve my constant state of anxiety, which, after academic stress and agoraphobia, was at fever pitch. Watching the black-and-white TV upstairs every once in a while did work temporary wonders, since a person cannot focus on two things at once—in this case, WCCO-TV programming and my anxiety. But when the distractions ended, and I could think of no further excuses to stay up, the anxious demons descended.

One night was especially bad. As usual, I took a long walk all around the neighborhood, hoping the exercise would release soothing biochemicals and help me to relax. That night's regimen began on an upbeat note: I was able to tune in the Chicago Bears preseason game on the portable radio I'd taken along for the walk. Hearing the announcer provided me a familiar voice, always a welcome relief to someone in whom aloneness played such a central role in keeping anxiety at bay. But not even the gridiron exploits of what would become a championship team that season provided lasting relief once I switched off the radio.

Back at the house, Diana had already descended the stairs into the basement and now slumbered peacefully. I went inside and climbed into bed beside her. Would my lengthy stroll be enough to provide the respite of sweet sleep? At the very least, I could try not to think about my anxiety.

In the world of mental health there exists a phenomenon called the "elephant-in-the-room effect." [WHITE elephant is an often tacky gift begging to be regifted. PINK elephant is the hallucination of someone drunken. The more accurate term is "elephant in the room" (no color attached)]. It's rooted in the idea that if you tell someone not to think of an elephant, that's all they'll be able to think about. Deliberate mental (and emotional) suppression doesn't work. (Remember "thought-stopping"?)

Psychologist Susan David refers to emotional suppression as "bottling." In *Emotional Agility* David writes, "Bottlers try to unhook by pushing emotions to the side [or underground] and getting on with things. They're likely to shove away unwanted feelings because those feelings are uncomfortable or distracting."[2]

Many bottlers try to "fix" their negative thoughts and behaviors by thinking positive thoughts. While there's nothing wrong with trying to look on the bright side of life, for bottlers this approach is simply a ruse. "Unfortunately, trying *not* to do something takes a surprising amount of mental bandwidth," writes Susan David. "And research shows that attempting to minimize or ignore thoughts and emotions only serves to amplify them."[3] (This is one reason a therapeutic technique called "thought-stopping" is going out of vogue.)

In commenting on the elephant-in-the-room effect, Susan David provides this helpful analogy: "Any dieter who has dreamed of chocolate cake and French fries understands the counterproductive nature of 'just don't think about it' and other avoidance strategies."[4] The outcome of trying to stuff, or "bottle," our emotions and anxieties is predictable: "It feels like it gives us control, but it actually denies us control."[5]

At first, bottling may feel successful. But it doesn't bode well over time. The repressed thoughts and emotions "inevitably surface in unintended ways, a process that psychologists call 'emotional leakage.'"[6] Like crafty groundhogs, those thoughts "have just gone underground—ready to pop back up at any time, and usually with surprising and inappropriate intensity ginned up by the containment pressure they've been under."[7]

Now, don't overplay this hand and begin obsessing about "what might happen" if you don't relieve the emotional/mental pressure. If you're a bottler—which most of us who've danced with anxiety disorders are—the eventual breaking of your emotional dam is not going to lead to some kind of long-feared psychotic breakdown wherein you "go crazy" and do something worthy of the psych ward or state penitentiary. Rather, increased anxiety itself is the main symptom of your suppression. Part of your healing protocol should involve therapy to help begin releasing this unhealthy pressure. In my experience, the flow of tears under the guidance of a qualified counselor or therapist is a good indicator that you're heading in the right direction.

The veracity of the elephant-in-the-room effect was proven yet again that night in Minnesota. Trying to get myself not to think about my anxiety was just as effective as trying to not think about an elephant. The walk hadn't worked, and racing anxious thoughts raged against all hope for a good night's sleep. As I lay there, wide-awake yet desperately craving rest, another unwelcome phenomenon rose to the surface of my turbulent mind.

The psychological phenomenon known as depersonalization can manifest itself in various ways. One manifestation involves a feeling that a person is not completely in touch with his or her mind or body. In my case, sometimes while driving I would begin feeling as though my arms and hands were not as connected to my body as they should be. I use the word *feeling* in this instance, because at no time did I ever believe this had actually taken place. But the borderline subconscious fear that it might happen escalated the depersonalizing effect, playing into a vicious cycle.

The worst night in Minnesota found me battling another form of depersonalization: fear of an out-of-body experience. (My admittedly cursory research into out-of-body experiences leaves me persuaded that most such episodes involve an alteration in carbon dioxide levels, a conclusion that seems to correlate with specific panic and anxiety symptoms. Still, there is much to learn.)

Misery may love company, but I'd have walked cross-country on my knuckles to not experience any form of depersonalization again. I did, however (brace yourself for this), survive every one of these episodes intact. Now that I have a better understanding of how related the mind and body really are, I seldom think of depersonalization. (That's just a little teaser that in the matter of progress, this book doesn't end anywhere close to where it began.)

A bit more about depersonalization, which is a familiar companion to many anxiety sufferers: What I've described may not meet the full criteria for the actual depersonalization-derealization disorder. In some ways, my experience with the phenomenon may have involved my fixation on control. What if this distancing of self from body morphed into some kind of irreversible state of mind?

To help clarify the clinical condition, Mayo Clinic provides a comprehensive description of depersonalization-derealization disorder. I'm going to quote it here, because I want any readers suffering from such episodes to understand more about it, and understand that while it may be uncomfortable, it's not deadly. Most important, know that it is highly treatable.

According to MayoClinic.org:

> The experience and feelings of the disorder can be difficult to describe. Worry about "going crazy" can cause you to become preoccupied with checking that you exist and determining what's actually real.

Mayo Clinic separates symptoms as follows:

Symptoms of *depersonalization* include:

▶ Feelings that you're an outside observer of your thoughts, feelings, your body or parts of your body, perhaps as if you were floating in air above yourself

▶ Feeling like a robot or that you're not in control of your speech or movements

▶ The sense that your body, legs, or arms appear distorted, enlarged or shrunken, or that your head is wrapped in cotton

▶ Emotional or physical numbness of your senses or responses to the world around you

▶ A sense that your memories lack emotion, and that they may or may not be your own memories

Symptoms of *derealization* include:

▶ Feelings of being alienated from or unfamiliar with your surroundings, perhaps as if you're living in a movie

▶ Feeling emotionally disconnected from people you care about, as if you were separated by a glass wall

▶ Surroundings that appear distorted, blurry, colorless, two-dimensional or artificial, or a heightened awareness and clarity of your surroundings

▶ Distortions in perception of time, such as recent events feeling like the distant past

▶ Distortions of distance and the size and shape of objects[8]

If you're experiencing some of these symptoms as part of your anxiety disorder package, know that you're not alone. As the saying goes, it is what it is. The good news is that it doesn't have to be that way for long.

TWELVE

HOPE ACROSS THE BRIDGE

The biggest challenge of my seminary experience now lay on the horizon. I would not be able to claim my diploma without fulfilling the program's "field school" requirement. Located in a Chicago suburb, the seminary's remote training center would provide us with hands-on evangelistic training. We'd be knocking on doors, visiting "interests," preaching, and more. The practical aspects were immense—and I was practically freaking out at the thought of spending a dozen weeks seventy miles away from Diana in the nation's third-largest city. It seemed more than ironic that the training center was located not more than a few miles from where I'd endured my panic attack on the Dan Ryan Expressway Maybe I'd end up baptizing the very nurse who'd injected me with a sedative that night in Jackson Park more than a decade earlier!

The whole thing seemed impossible. Diana had a full-time job, and expecting her to submit a leave request or even her resignation to accompany her "wimpy" husband to Chicago was out of the question. If only I could beat this thing! If only . . .

During this time I was still receiving a monthly stipend from my denominational sponsor and potential future employer. I knew they would be less than pleased to find out that their investment might not pay off after all. I decided that rather than tell them I was leaving altogether, I would request a leave of absence. I don't remember if my excuse revolved around academic burnout, career uncertainty, or something else. Nor do I know exactly what prompted the gracious response that I received in return. Whatever their rationale, my sponsors were OK with me taking a break. The Windy City would have to be converted to Christianity without me.

So I was off the hook—and without a master's degree. The decision also meant the discontinuance of my denominational funding, so I asked for an increase in hours at the furniture store. It would be for just a little while, until I could make progress on my travel issue. None of this was made public, of course. The charade continued, although it seemed clear that not everyone who asked about the situation was buying my flimsy responses. The good news was that most inquirers didn't really care enough about my future to press the issue.

We moved out of the university bungalow and into a leaky farmhouse adjacent to the St. Joseph River. The view was stunning, which was more than offset by the abysmal dirt road and the house's termite infestation. Worse still, the place was located some seven miles from the furniture store. But it was the only thing we could afford rent-wise, and since Diana worked nearby the furniture store, we could travel together to and from work. For those times when we had conflicting schedules, well, I'd figure something out.

When it comes to launching a full-out assault on anxiety, several things can stand in the way. Dr. Michael Tompkins sheds light on this area in his book *OCD: A Guide for the Newly Diagnosed.* Although his focus is obsessive-compulsive disorder, a section subtitled "Shame, Fear, and Denial" provides insight applicable to all anxiety disorders sufferers:

> Often, people with obsessive-compulsive disorder (OCD) know that something is amiss but are reluctant to seek help. This is unfortunate because we know that most people who seek and participate fully in treatment improve, sometimes greatly.

> There are a number of reasons you may be reluctant to seek treatment for your OCD. You may feel ashamed by what you think of as the bizarre nature of your obsessive thoughts. You may believe that having the thoughts means you are an immoral or terrible person so you feel ashamed and reluctant to tell people about these thoughts. You may have tried many times to stop washing or checking rituals because you know the washing or checking is excessive, but you feel powerless to stop. It's not easy to tell someone that you are aware your behavior doesn't make sense but that you have to do it anyway.[1]

Tompkins digs a little deeper:

> In addition to the shame you feel, you may be afraid to seek help for your OCD, fearing that you will lose your job, marriage, or children if people find out you

have OCD. A former client told me that she suffered for years with obsessions that she might molest her children. She did not tell her parents or even her husband about these thoughts because she feared that they would tell the authorities and they would take away her children. You may have read something about the treatment of your OCD, particularly about exposure, and now you worry that this will only make your symptoms worse or truly create the catastrophe you are working so hard to prevent. Fear, like shame, may cause you to attempt to suppress your obsessions (try to keep them out of your mind), which only makes things worse. As you try to not think about the disgusting or terrifying thoughts or images that come into your mind, you realize that they are coming with greater frequency and intensity. This, in turn, makes you believe that you might be going crazy or that what you fear may indeed be true.[2]

These comments accurately reflect much of what I thought and felt during the time I was in bondage to anxiety disorders. You may be experiencing them right now. Please know that with the right kind of treatment, they can become a distant memory, just as they have for me. It will take courage, but your life will never be the same.

All was not lost during the time of my vocational hiatus. I was still making some progress with Dr. Baker, and a friend and I had started work on a collection of skits for publication. To our great joy, the manuscript was accepted, and the book became a strong seller in its market. A follow-up volume ensued, and it sold well too.

Somehow word got around that Randy Fishell might be available to fill a youth pastor position, something I'd always thought of as my dream job. Inquiries came from a variety of locations—Chicago, Sacramento, and elsewhere. I played a shameful game, expressing interest at first but always declining in the end. Sure, it felt good that someone considered my life and skills valuable, and maybe this all helped keep me from tumbling into a dark abyss of irreversible despair. After all, it *did* feel good to be wanted. But I knew any potential employer would not want a staff member who couldn't drive alone even a few miles to attend a teen's birthday party or help mend their broken heart. I would be worthless as a youth pastor. For now, at least I was good at selling mattresses and floor coverings. Why, I had even helped increase sales by taping a TV commercial airing during *Wheel of Fortune*. "When you lie down on our newest pillow-top mattress, you'll feel like you're sleeping on a cloud!" I informed viewers with a sweeping gesture.

That made me worth something, didn't it?

One day I received a phone call from a former seminary professor, Dr. Gruesbeck. "Randy, I want to talk to you about something. Do you have a minute?"

I held Dr. Gruesbeck in high regard, so I was eager to find out what was on his mind.

"I'm retirement age, but I don't want to just sit around," he explained. "There's a church in Seattle that's asked me to come and be their pastor. They also have a position open for someone to work with the nearby students at the University of Washington." He went on and then asked, "Would you consider joining me in Seattle?"

Then he tossed in this as an added incentive: "Oh, and

you'll be able to finish the last requirements for your degree from out there."

I was stunned. I could at last claim my Master of Divinity degree without moving to Chicago as the seminary curriculum prescribed? Dr. Gruesbeck explained that the only other option for finishing my degree's requirements was a seminary-run program that just happened to be about ten miles south of Seattle! I'd go there first, finish my degree, and then join Dr. Gruesbeck in Seattle's Green Lake area immediately afterward as an assistant pastor for youth and young adults.

We talked a bit more, and of course I told Dr. Gruesbeck that Diana and I would pray about the possibility. Accepting the position would not only place me back in the center of my chosen vocation but would also move us up a rung or two on the socioeconomic ladder. This had become more important, since Diana's pregnancy test had come back positive. If you've ever had a kid, you know they don't come cheap.

Deep down, I knew that this might be my last chance to avoid making furniture and carpet sales a lifelong profession. Not that home furnishings is a vocational wasteland—it's just that I'd worked so hard to become something else. Surely, I could figure out a way to make it work in Seattle.

Over the next few nights I rationalized to the point of exhaustion as to how a person who couldn't drive alone could serve as a pastor and mentor to teens and young adults. I studied a map of Seattle and convinced myself that I'd be able to fake my way until I got better.

Yes, that was it. Someday, probably soon, I'd get better. After all, I hadn't *always* been this way. Why, with enough hard work, it was a given that I'd be able to put this whole thing behind me once and for all.

Suddenly, I remembered the brochure I'd sent away for after I'd heard the woman from the TERRAP agoraphobia recovery program speak on the radio. I pulled the brochure from a desk drawer and scanned the list of locations where the program was offered. My eyes grew wide when I saw Seattle included on the relatively short list. Surely this whole thing was nothing other than the convergence of divine providences!

"I think we'd better give this a shot," I told Diana a few days later, and she agreed. We'd first need to have a successful interview with the church board in Seattle, so Dr. Gruesbeck made the arrangements for Diana and I to fly there after he was settled in.

As the plane rolled to a stop at Sea-Tac International Airport, I glanced out the aircraft's window. The first thing my eyes landed on was the gigantic tail of an adjacent airliner. It featured an Eskimo and the words "Alaska Airlines." A feeling that I'd just arrived at the edge of the world washed over me. How much farther could I possibly be from my super-constricted comfort zone back in Michigan?

To my chagrin, included in the weekend's interview process would be a "test run" to see how I related to the young adults. This was to take place at someone's house where an after-church potluck took place every week. Walking into the home on North Aurora Avenue, I felt as if the house lights had just been shut down and a spotlight fully thrust on this pastoral staff candidate and his wife. What song and dance should I perform to impress everyone? Should I recite the book of Revelation from memory? Whip out pictures of all the youth whose lives I'd impacted for eternity? All of this self-focus was strictly in my own mind, of course. There may have been a few curious young adult onlookers, but most of them were far too invested in eating baked macaroni and cheese than in peering my direction.

Echoes of another seminary professor's counsel surfaced. "Randy, I've been looking at the results of your Readiness for Ministry test, and I have a concern. You score very low in the area of social comfort and interaction."

At the time, I'd blown it off as just another useless bit of information. Now I knew there was something to it. This was before the term *social anxiety* had come into vogue, but here it was on full display. Did the young adults and others in the room know that I was about as comfortable as a weed in an herbicide factory? Probably not, but I would've done most anything to be called out of the room for an extended period of time.

"So, um, what would you like to see a pastor for young adults bring to the church?" I finally awkwardly asked a college student.

She smiled and responded politely, but I could tell that, she too, felt uncomfortable. The whole set-up was fake. Me, a total stranger, trying to act friendly while probing for meaningful input. It was doomed to fail from the start. Thankfully, Diana was elsewhere in the room just being her reserved but engaging self, and that saved my potluck train appearance from going too far off the rails.

The following evening, after the potluck's hostess had expressed her personal reservations about my candidacy, the church board voted to invite me to join the church staff after completing field school in nearby Kent, Washington. It was the beginning of another ending for me.

The quest to never be far from home base continued upon our arrival in Kent. I breathed a sigh of relief when I discovered that the complex where we'd take up temporary residence, Quail Ridge Apartments, was within walking distance of the training center. We'd be there from September through December, and then move on to Seattle in January to take up my official duties at the church in the Green Lake district.

Occasionally, my ministry partner, Delwin, and I had to make a trek somewhere in the area to follow up on someone's inquiry about spiritual matters. It was always an uncomfortable adventure for me, not because of Delwin, but because I would be out of my safety zone. But at least there would be someone else in the car with me, and that helped stave off major panic symptoms. But anxiety was ever-present, and getting back home was always a relief.

December came along, and with it a short graduation service. I had finally earned my master's degree—all without having to drive anywhere alone. Diana knew that I was battling anxiety, but I still hadn't shared with her just how debilitating my condition really was. Oh, in a way, she could understand certain aspects. With her own fear of flying, it had been a major victory when she'd flown with me for the job interview. As for my own struggle, I'd been able to dance my way around the issue for the past several years with such finesse that my handicap had not become an overarching discussion in our marriage.

Our prayers now revolved around finding a home in Seattle. I knew that it would have to be located close to the church, but what were the chances of finding anything affordable in the relatively high-rent Green Lake district?

"Look at this," Diana said one day after searching the Seattle *Post-Intelligencer* classified ads section yet another time. It was an ad for a little bungalow rental about a mile from the University of Washington, and less than a mile from the church in Green Lake in another direction. (I'd have responsibilities in both locations.)

We called the landlord, who agreed to show us the place. The little house on Northeast 76th Street turned out to be the perfect answer to our—OK, *my*—needs. Sure, the little basement room that would become my study reverberated incessantly with the sound of nearby Interstate 5, but who cared? I breathed a huge sigh of relief as we wrote a check for the first month's rent plus deposit. Pushing the shame ever deeper inside me, we soon found ourselves unloading the moving van and settling into our humble but perfectly situated house. Such was my denial that I began to think, *Why, I might never have to get into my car again!* I falsely assumed that my ministry creativity would be so irresistible that everyone would flock to me rather than vice versa.

By this time, Diana was just a few weeks away from giving birth to our first son. When a few church leaders began questioning why their new hire didn't seem to be venturing out to meet anyone, I had multiple excuses at hand: "Got to take Diana to lots of pediatrician appointments"…"I'm putting a master ministry plan together"…and "Trying to get settled into our new home" all worked to my advantage—for a few weeks. The church elders began to show signs of hair loss from scratching their heads.

By now the stress of change began to take an even greater toll on my behavior. It was getting harder and harder to fend off panic symptoms, even with Diana in tow as my "safe person."

One weekend, a wealthy church member had invited the young adults on a yachting trip. Obviously, the new pastor for young adults was expected to get on board. The idea of being in the middle of a body of water with no ability to get help should I require it cast the lot in favor of finding yet another excuse. "Um, I'm going to plan a great event and have it waiting for you when you dock," I told everyone. At this, a leading church member told another one sarcastically within my hearing, "I guess he's waiting for something really exciting to happen."

My cheeks grew warm with embarrassment. Who could blame them? It looked like the church had made a major mistake in hiring me, and nobody could figure out why I wasn't doing anything. I was, in fact, pulling together a ministry "action plan." The problem was, it was based more on my dysfunctional needs than the needs of the church's youth and young adults.

Over the next few months, my creativity and fresh style of preaching helped to salvage my reputation. When Dr. Gruesbeck went away for several weeks that summer, I filled the pulpit each week, and my messages were a hit. Earlier clouds of doubt filling the church members' minds gave way to the promise of a young pastor who was energizing the congregation. *Maybe somehow he'll work out after all,* at least some of them reasoned.

About this time, Diana and I organized a drama troupe consisting of high schoolers and college students. When our first performance virtually packed the usually sparsely attended service, even my strongest detractor searched me out for a compliment. "Randy," he said, "just look around this place. Something is happening!" Apparently, even he was beginning to think that perhaps the person they thought was a poor excuse for a youth and young adult pastor might actually be some kind of church-growth genius in disguise.

They were wrong. Yes, some good things *were* happening at the church. But one of my titles was chaplain to the University of Washington, and by midsummer of my first year in that role, I'd still not set foot on campus. Even a mile away was too far for me to travel alone down constricted city streets.

Shame on me.

In the 1970s, a psychiatrist in the United States was achieving some therapeutic success with agoraphobic patients via his own recovery protocols. Dr. Arthur Boydston Hardy was a California psychiatrist who specialized in treating people with symptoms of anxiety. According to its website, "TERRAP (a conjunction of the terms TERRitorial and APprehension) is a national organization founded by Dr. Arthur B. Hardy

[*176*]

in 1975. During that time, psychiatrists were trained to focus on discussing early childhood traumas, family dynamics, and marital issues, and Dr. Hardy followed these protocols. Although his patients did find some of the connections interesting, it did not seem to relieve them of their anxiety symptoms or their phobic avoidances. As a result of his own frustration with his patients' progress, Dr. Hardy decided to put together a program that incorporated education, relaxation training, cognitive behavioral therapy, and exposure therapy, and he put his research in a manual that was easy to read, understand, and implement. Over time, Dr. Hardy found that by providing his patients with specific techniques and gradual exposures, they were soon relieved of their anxiety symptoms.

As a result of this success in the field, Dr. Hardy founded The Phobia Society, which is now the Anxiety Disorders of America Association, where he is considered one of the pioneers in phobia treatment.[3]

When he died in 1991, his obituary in the *New York Times* was titled, "Arthur B. Hardy, 78, Psychiatrist Who Treated a Fear of Going Out." According to that piece, "Dr. Hardy . . . promoted a new treatment for agoraphobia that helped thousands of patients across the nation. . . . Agoraphobia, a fear of being in open or public places that is so intense that victims can be effectively confined to their homes, was renamed *territorial apprehension* by Dr. Hardy.

Dissatisfied with the results of classical psychoanalysis in treating the condition, Dr. Hardy broke from his Freudian training. He drew instead on the concepts of Dr. Arnold Lazarus and Dr. Joseph Wolpe at Stanford University in using behavior techniques like relaxation, de-sensitization, assertiveness training, gradual explora-tion and group support to free patients of their anxieties.

Reports on Dr. Hardy's work in the news media and his television appearances drew 50,000 requests from people seeking help, as well as inquiries from therapists wanting to learn the new treatment.[4]

Dr. Hardy's TERRAP program was the one I'd heard James Dobson and his guest talking about on *Focus on the Family* a few years earlier. A little research revealed that not only was there an affiliate in nearby Bellevue, Washington, but its organizer was none other than Dr. Hardy's very own daughter. She facilitated the enroll-ment process and was the connecting link between cli-ents and a local clinical psychologist who would be lead-ing the weekly TERRAP meetings.

Could TERRAP help me to deal my agoraphobia a death blow? When a source of funding came through enabling me to attend the high-priced sessions, my hope was rekindled. Perhaps I could become the post-er boy for the organization's successful treatment of agoraphobia!

Getting to Bellevue meant crossing the then-narrow and harrowing (to me) Highway 520 bridge across Lake Washington. In most ways, Seattle freeways are no dif-ferent than those found in any other major U.S. city, including Chicago, where I'd suffered my first intense panic attack. Any such travel was usually accompanied by varying degrees of anxiety, even with my safe person riding shotgun.

The evening of the first meeting found Diana and

our infant son packed into our Ford Tempo making our way across the Lake Washington Bridge toward Bellevue. Upon our arrival, as introductions were made, I was pleasantly surprised to see that not only were the attendees "normal" folks, but a high percentage appeared to be working professionals. *Where are all the weirdoes?* I wondered.

As we shared openly, I discovered that the challenges represented exceeded the boundaries of agoraphobia. One woman hoped to increase her assertiveness at work, while a gentleman on the opposite side of the room had a fear of using public restrooms. As for agoraphobia itself, I related to one older gentleman who owned not one but two classic 1950's-era Thunderbirds, but couldn't drive either of them anywhere alone.

As promised in the literature, the program involved a variety of techniques aimed at slowly-but-surely diminishing the drama associated with irrational fears. These tools included "thought-stopping," relaxation techniques, systematic desensitization (gradually exposing oneself to the toxic stimuli) and a bevy of other self-help activities.

After faithfully attending the weekly meetings for two months, I "graduated" with high hopes that soon I would indeed become a TERRAP success story.

I didn't. Was it because I simply hadn't tried hard enough? Was I less motivated to recover than I thought? Why in the world couldn't I seem to make any progress?

So does the TERRAP program work? As with any recovery program, from alcoholism to pornography, the theory is usually sound. Undoubtedly TERRAP has many success stories in their files. More relevant than the question "Does it work?" may be the question, "Can *any* recovery program guarantee success, lasting or otherwise, for every client?" The answer, of course, is no. There are simply too many variables, from degree of dysfunction to personal biochemistry to level of commitment and endless other factors. While I found the program's recovery theory credible, for me, putting it into practice seemed too overwhelming and time-consuming. A few weeks after the last meeting, I was no closer to feeling the weight of anxiety and agoraphobia lift from my shoulders than before I'd begun the TERRAP program.

In my mind, this was simply more evidence that I was not "man enough" to face and conquer such a determined enemy as agoraphobia. I just didn't have what it took the way other people did. I was too weak to "buck up" and get on with my life, even after I'd been handed a golden ticket called TERRAP.

But I could hardly make progress by tuning in to such a negative stream of consciousness. There had to be a solution just around the next corner. Time! Yes, that was it—I just needed a little more time to put everything I'd learned in TERRAP into practice. Maybe next week, after the regional pastors meeting was over. Or next month, when my senior pastor returned and I'd turn the pulpit back over to him—then I could focus on recovery.

And I really did try. Often, I'd find a quiet spot in the church, lie down, and do systematic relaxation exercises to help reduce my stress and anxiety levels. "Let your jaw relax . . . now raise your chin to your chest and let it fall back . . ." The man on the cassette tape (yeah, I know, what is a "cassette tape"?) did his best to help me reset my tension threshold, and I usually did feel a little better after each head-to-toe relaxation session. But nothing really changed, at least not for long. Every day, anxiety manifested itself in tight stomach muscles and a continuing inability to back out of my driveway and head down Interstate 5 alone. The relentless humming of thousands of commuters' vehicles just over the freeway's embankment was a constant reminder of my own failure. But at least I could walk to the church, something I did regularly, counting and clicking my teeth along the way.

THIRTEEN

TRUE CONFESSION

Diana had been eight months pregnant when we'd moved to the Northwest in September. It was now July of the following year, and she was going stir-crazy.

Early on, we'd agreed that if possible, Diana would be a "stay at home mom." Adding to the usual daily mother-hood drain was the fact that our precious firstborn usual-ly slept in fifteen-minute stages, the balance being filled with a variety of mommy-demanding activities. If any-one were ever truly sleepless in Seattle, it was my dear wife. She desperately needed a diversion from changing diapers and photocopying church bulletins.

What she needed more than anything was what some affectionately refer to as "me time." Not as in "me," her husband, but as in her fleeing the premises without me.

Problem incoming.

Diana had earned her undergraduate degree in radio broadcasting and had worked for both a National Public Radio affiliate and commercial radio stations. Now an-other form of media caught her attention.

"So they're holding this workshop on how to be in a TV commercial," she informed me. It seemed that a company specializing in such things was holding an event in downtown Seattle, and she wanted to attend. Alone. As in without me.

My dysfunction had escalated to the point where I'd pretty much glued myself to Diana, my safe person. It's hard to say who was more dependent on her presence: our infant son or her husband. But really, come on! I now lived in a big city where I knew hardly anyone. Who could help me if, well, something bad happened? No, I needed to be within "reaching distance" of my security blanket—I mean, safe person. Oh, sure, the whole attachment thing had gotten a little more cumbersome with a child in the picture, but I creatively painted a deceptive picture for others of a husband fully dedicated to being available to his wife and child at all times. After all, this was a whole new experience for us, wasn't it?

But now along came the TV ad workshop. How could I bend reality this time to accommodate my needs? I'd have to think fast. Or had the time come to put some of what I'd learned in TERRAP into practice?

I mustered my courage and called a fellow attendee. "Hey, Fernando, this is Randy from the TERRAP group. Um, I was wondering if you might want to, um, come over next Sunday and watch the Seahawks game at my house," I awkwardly invited. Watching a football game at a pastor's house—a nondrinking, nonsmoking, vegetarian at that—is hardly an invitation to party paradise. Still, it seemed worth a shot.

Fernando hesitated before declining my invitation. His fear of using a public restroom may have included restrooms in unfamiliar homes as well, I really don't know. Or perhaps he was simply wondering why someone he hardly knew would be inviting him to watch a football game together. Either way, it was a no-go.

Growing more desperate (I realize how absurd this all seems to someone who's never experienced panic), I called Rick, a young adult at church with whom I'd become good friends. I'd confided a bit in him about my situation, and he agreed to come over and spend a little time with me on Sunday morning.

The day arrived, and Rick pulled up as Diana was leaving the house with a friend who'd picked her up. It would be Randy, Rick, and an eight-month-old crying baby for the next few hours. At least, that's how it was supposed to go. After about an hour of mind-numbing boredom, Rick told me he had to leave. I don't remember where he said he was going, but I'm sure that just about anywhere would have been more fulfilling than babysitting an infant *and* the child's father. That may seem at least mildly humorous, but it is a shame-filled, accurate reflection of what was taking place on the north side of Seattle that morning.

"Hey, no need to rush off, Rick," I said, sweating bullets.

"Well, thanks, but I'll see you at church," he said and headed toward the front door. A couple of minutes later the taillights of his souped-up Plymouth Duster disappeared around the corner. It didn't take long for the panic to sweep in. There was only one safe person in the entire city of Seattle, and she was downtown taking a workshop in Smith Tower. Fear outweighing shame, I grabbed Tyler, along with his car seat and baby stroller, and headed for our car parked in the driveway. Fighting panic all the way, I set out for nearby downtown Seattle.

As I neared our exit, a horrible reality set in: the Seahawks were playing at home! The Kingdome was just a few blocks from Smith Tower; what would be the chances of finding a parking spot anywhere nearby?

I glanced in the back seat at our innocent bundle of joy. How could I be such a mess and call myself a responsible father? And what if my panic grew to the point where I fainted? What would happen to the little boy in the back seat? All these thoughts accomplished was to kick my panic into overdrive. Heart pounding, dizziness creeping in, I glanced at a nearby parking garage. I wheeled in, knowing that the odds of finding an empty slot during game time were slim to none.

Suddenly, I saw a parking attendant waving at me in the cavernous facility. What to my wondering eyes should appear but one lonely parking space! I cranked the steering wheel, pulled into the space, and paid the attendant. Miracles never cease.

I pulled the baby stroller out of the trunk and strapped our son into it. As the Seahawks played football not far distant, my own goal was to find Diana and reassure myself that a safe person was finally close at hand.

Inside the Smith Tower lobby, I spotted a sign indicating where the TV ad training workshop was being held. I pushed the stroller over to the elegant but antiquated elevators and pushed the button that would carry us upward toward relief from my mental anguish. When we reached our floor, the elevator doors opened, and I pushed the stroller out onto the old linoleum floor. Whether Diana had spotted us through a glass window, or if she just

happened to be in the hallway at that time I do not recall. Either way, her eyes met mine, and her shoulders
slumped. I had ruined her getaway. "What's going on?"
she asked sharply.

I bit my lip and said, "Um, I was getting nervous."

She said nothing.

"Look, I'm sorry, OK?" I paused, then asked, "What's
wrong?"

As if I had no clue.

She hesitated, then said, "It all just feels so . . . *clingy*."

I hung my head as she returned to the workshop room.
Father and baby son wandered the hallway until, at last,
the workshop was over. The short ride home, with Diana
now in the passenger seat, seemed to take forever.

"Sure, I can meet you for lunch on Tuesday," my friend
Brad told me over the phone. "Where?"

"We can sit and eat across from the church," I suggested. Green Lake itself would provide a soothing backdrop
for the bomb I was about to drop on my church member,
ministry supporter, and friend. I needed to tell someone
about my situation, and Brad was my chosen confidant.

Unlike so many Seattle days, Tuesday was picture-per-
fect. Brad, a printing sales representative, pulled up with
his sunroof fully retracted. "This is what Seattle in summer is all about!" he said, smiling broadly. Soon we were
seated on the lawn near the lake, sack lunches in hand. At
last I began my little speech.

"Um, Brad," I began slowly, "I want to share with you
something about me that I've pretty much kept a secret.
Rick knows a little bit about it, but not too much." Perhaps Brad expected me to say that I was subversively

a Chicago Cubs fan living in Seattle Mariners' territory (which I was). That would've been a lot easier than what I was about to share.

"So what's up?" Brad asked.

I sucked in a deep breath and continued. "By now you may have noticed that I'm not getting around the city as much as church members would like."

"Yeah, I think it's fair to say that some of us are a little baffled," Brad admitted.

I nodded and simply said, "That's because I have agoraphobia."

Brad set down his sandwich and asked, "What's agoraphobia?"

"Well, it's kind of complicated, but the bottom line is that I can't really drive anywhere alone. When I do, I have panic attacks."

Brad happens to have a higher-than-average IQ, so it didn't take him long to begin filling in quite a few blanks.

"If Diana is around, things are sort of OK," I continued. "I know it sounds totally stupid and it's probably really hard for you to understand."

"So you're saying Diana has to go everywhere with you?"

"Yeah, pretty much," I said softly.

"Wow, and there's a baby at home now. This must be taking a real toll on her."

I had no counterargument with which to deflect Brad's painful assertion. I went on to tell him about how hard I'd tried to deal with the issue, including the TERRAP program, and that I hoped he'd support any continuing efforts to overcome my challenges.

"Well, of course I'll support you," he quickly responded. "This does explain a lot," he added. "So what are you thinking about the future?"

I didn't *want* to think about the future, but I finally responded. "I don't know for sure. I'm going to keep trying to practice what I learned in TERRAP. But I just don't know." With a recent cross-country move, a new baby, a new job, and battling panic disorder and agoraphobia, the stress was intense. Had my obsessive-compulsive disorder symptoms risen to past levels during this time, it would have seemed unbearable. The other anxiety factors were so dominant that OCD had taken a back seat. Oh, I was always counting and clicking my teeth, but most of the time I was simply unaware that I was doing either.

But now Brad knew, and that provided a little relief.

We chatted further and then got ready to head our separate directions. Suddenly Brad looked at me and said, "Randy, thanks for the honor of your confidence."

As I watched Brad drive off that sunny Tuesday, I felt a slight surge of hope. Somehow sharing the burden made it a little easier. Sometime later Brad called me on the phone. "Randy, you know that agoraphobia thing you told me about? Well, believe it or not, I finally made sense of something. See, something has been going on with my wife. She's been having a really hard time leaving the house. Now I get it." He paused and added, "Thanks again for confiding in me."

I was happy that my confession had made a difference. I only hoped that Brad's wife would have more success in dealing with agoraphobia than I'd had.

As the Seattle winter approached, I knew the time had

come to make a decision. I could continue the charade, or I could admit that this youth and university pastor gig just wasn't working out. The constant knot in my stomach was a determining factor.

"Dr. Gruesbeck," I said to my former professor-turned-senior pastor, "I've made a decision."

"About what?" he asked nonchalantly.

"My future here."

He looked up from his desk. "Oh?" I'd already hinted that things didn't seem to be going in the most positive direction, and that I'd been thinking about the future. As a result, what came next was not a complete surprise.

"I've talked to Diana, and we think it's probably best to leave Seattle."

"I see," the man responded coolly. I couldn't really blame him for feeling a little betrayed. He'd worked hard to get me to Green Lake and defended my less-than-optimal performance more than once. But I literally knew in my gut that I needed to get out.

The good pastor asked me to stay on, and I think he really meant it when he said, "I need you, Randy." That made it doubly difficult to tell him that I'd made a firm decision to leave in February, just a few weeks away.

With the transitional die cast, Diana and I began thinking about what vocational direction I should pursue. I enjoyed writing, but I didn't like the idea of starving, so I began sending out résumés to various publishing companies.

One day Diana and I stopped by a local Christian bookstore to browse. Spinning the establishment's magazine rack around, I spotted one of my favorites: *Discipleship Journal*, published by an organization called the

Navigators, based in Colorado Springs, Colorado. I pointed to the magazine and told Diana with a smile, "You know what I'd like to do? I'd like to be an assistant editor at *Discipleship Journal*." I'd specifically said *assistant* editor because I reasoned that such a position would involve minimal travel, unlike a senior editorial position.

That passing comment about my "dream position" would come back to haunt me sooner that I could have imagined.

A couple of weeks after sending out résumés, our home phone rang. It was a book editorial supervisor from Group Publishing, also based in Colorado.

"We got your résumé, and it seems like you may have some things we're looking for, Randy," the person on the other end of the line said. "We need a book editor here at Group. Would you be interested in taking an editorial test for the position?"

Sure I would. After all, I was about to become jobless, so editing books seemed better than filling out unemployment forms.

"We'll send you a test manuscript for you to work on. Just send it back to me when you're done," the man instructed.

When the manuscript arrived, I whacked away at it until it hardly resembled the original product. I slipped it back into the mailbox (this was before editable PDFs or the cloud had arrived on the scene) and waited for a call back from Colorado. To my great joy, the same person who'd called previously soon called back.

"You did a great job, Randy," the man said. "Maybe a little *too* great, because we do like to leave the author's original voice in place. But you did really well." He went on to say that there'd be one more phone interview before proceeding, and that took place a few days later. Everything sailed smoothly until he asked me one question: "Do you work well under stress?"

I began perspiring. *Should I tell him what he wants to hear, or should I tell him the truth?* I wondered, my mind racing. I decided there was no point in faking it, so I responded as sincerely as I could. "I can't say that working under stress is a strong point for me," I said.

The interviewer paused before speaking. "I see," came the clearly disappointed reply. "Well, in that case, I think we'd better keep looking. It's been great getting to know you." Gainful employment had suddenly vanished in thin air.

A few days later my church office phone rang. "Susan, the senior editor at *Discipleship Journal* just called!" Diana excitedly told me. "They're looking for an assistant editor, and they just got your résumé. She wants you to call her right away!"

A little chill went up my spine. I remembered the off-handed comment I'd made a few weeks earlier about my "dream job." This had to be the direct hand of Providence at work.

"OK, I'll call her," I told Diana. Soon I was on the phone with Susan, listening to her describe the job opening. It seemed like a good fit.

"We need to do a little more talking here, but I'll call you back in a few days," Susan said after I expressed interest in the position.

A couple of days later, she called back. "We'd like you and Diana to fly out here to Colorado Springs to talk in person," Susan explained. "Would you be able to do that soon?" I told her that I'd call her back with our itinerary. I began sleuthing out airline tickets.

That night Diana and I lay in bed staring at the ceiling. Our firstborn slept peacefully in the bassinet next to us. After several minutes of silence, I spoke to Diana.

"Something about this just doesn't feel right," I said.

She paused, then said softly, "No, it doesn't."

How could either of us possibly think such a thought? Why, even my senior pastor had told me how this appeared to be a direct call from God! But all the outside signs could not override the inner conviction that going to Colorado Springs was the wrong thing to do.

Against all reason, I called Susan back the following day and declined the invitation to fly to Colorado. By turning down the opportunity to be further considered, had I hung up on God Himself? But then, if there really was a God out there somewhere, did He even care about my life? He'd certainly not fixed my anxiety issues. Did I actually have a reason to keep on believing? Either way, the phone call I'd just made had surely sealed my fate. What good could possibly lie ahead?

FOURTEEN

ON THE MOVE

Snoqualmie Pass in the Cascades during February can be downright dangerous. But here we were, a young family of three headed eastward out of Seattle and back to Michigan. I'd failed as a pastor, and climbing the mountain pass in the blinding snow seemed somehow symbolic of where my life appeared to be headed. We'd be staying that night in Walla Walla with a family friend, then continuing the several-days' journey back to my hometown.

The cities rolled by: Coeur d'Alene, Idaho; Billings, Montana; Sioux Falls, South Dakota. A little more than a year earlier we'd approached them from the opposite direction. How could so much have happened—and in the case of my recovery, *not* happened—in these past months?

Thankfully, both of our previous employers in Michigan had agreed to rehire us. Diana would work at the university bookstore until three o'clock in the afternoon, while I stayed home with Tyler and worked on a new book I was writing. Then, when Diana got home, I'd head off to the furniture store for a late-afternoon/evening shift.

Our temporary "home" was actually an upstairs bedroom in my parents' home. The plan was to stay there until we could find a place to rent. I'm sure they would've appreciated having something more stellar to announce in that year's Christmas newsletter than "Randy, Diana, and baby Tyler moved back into our house because Randy failed miserably as a pastor in Seattle." Maybe they'd at least find a more nuanced way to state it.

Setting the whole affair behind me wasn't as easy as I'd hoped. Nightmares and eventually chest pains landed me in the doctor's office. It turned out that I wasn't dying—a diagnosis I'd heard a hundred times before. But I knew that my body's chemistry—and life itself—was somehow badly out of balance.

Within a couple of months, we found a little house to rent near the university campus. Diana could walk to her work at the university bookstore, and the furniture store was only about a mile up the road, so I could drive the familiar highway alone with minimal discomfort.

One afternoon as I pushed Tyler in his stroller along a university street, I noticed a professor with whom I'd had a spat in the furniture store before I'd left for Seattle driving toward me. He was an arrogant man, and as a mutual acquaintance once told me, "He plays by his own set of rules."

Still, at some level, he somehow represented everything I wasn't: self-assured, smart, and successful. He sported a late-model car while I bumped along in a used Ford Tempo whose air-conditioner had long ago given up the ghost. I lifted my hand to wave at him, believing that somehow taking a proactive stance would unmistakably convey that I still possessed a measure of dignity. After all, didn't everyone within a three-state area know how Randy Fishell had failed at his chosen profession? Yes, surely everyone had heard that something had gone terribly wrong. An assertive gesture such as waving at the haughty professor would be an unmistakable signal that I was not ashamed.

He looked at me but did not return the wave. Was that a smug, knowing smile I saw splashed across his face as he passed? Yes, it must have been. He, like all the others, knew. Not everything, to be sure, but enough: Randy Fishell was a failure. I continued down the street, pushing the stroller and struggling to keep further shame at bay.

Years later, I discovered at least a partial explanation for how I felt that day. While there is no denying that I was experiencing a deep sense of failure, the idea that people were secretly celebrating my dilemma—or in most cases even remotely interested—was simply a self-deception. I'd fallen victim to what's known in some circles as the "spotlight effect."

In his book *You Are Not So Smart*, David McRaney explains the spotlight effect. Although his focus revolves around people in public settings, the effect can feel the same in various settings, such as pushing a baby stroller down the sidewalk. McRaney explains that when the conditions are right, "You think every little nuance of your behavior is under scrutiny by everyone else. . . . You can't help but be the center of your universe, and you find it difficult to gauge just how much other people are paying attention since you are paying attention to you all the time."[1] Of course they aren't, but you're convinced otherwise.

You spend so much time thinking about your own body, your own thoughts and behaviors [or failures, in my case], you begin to think other people must be noticing too. The research says they aren't, at least not nearly as much as you are.[2]

McRaney provides further perspective—and comfort—when he adds, "Fortunately, everyone else is just as egocentric, and they are just as convinced that they are being scrutinized."[3]

One of the great ironies of certain psychological (and physical) disorders is that even though they can prove so destructive, they can also bring certain "benefits." I'm not talking about the way a person becomes more sensitive to others' struggles (although that is true) or similar personal growth breakthroughs. There is a twisted phenomenon known as "secondary gain," which can help to keep a person rooted in dysfunction. An abstract on this subject includes this summary:

Secondary gain is defined as the advantage that occurs secondary to stated or real illness. Transition into the sick role may have some incidental secondary gains for patients. Types of secondary gain[s] include using illness for personal advantage, exaggerating symptoms, consciously using symptoms for gain, and unconsciously presenting symptoms with no physiological basis. These symptoms may contribute to the social breakdown syndrome and the patient's choice to remain in the sick role.[4]

You read that correctly: a person might *choose* to stay

sick because of certain advantages that outweigh the benefits of becoming healthy. For example, a person with tendonitis in their gas pedal foot might eventually relish the experience of being chauffeured here and there. Similarly, an individual with agoraphobia can grow to appreciate the social value of always having someone along for the ride, or not having to accept civic or church responsibilities because they can't attend meetings. Dr. Alice Boyles, author of *The Anxiety Toolkit* and a blogger for *Psychology Today*, provides further examples of secondary gain:

▶ A person with chronic pain does not really like spending time with their partner's friends. When the person is experiencing a lot of pain, their partner does not pressure them to go to social events as much.

▶ A client gets more encouragement and caring comments from their therapist the longer they stay distressed during sessions.

▶ Someone uses depression as an explanation for why they can't do something their partner wants, when they would find it hard even if they were not depressed. Their partner backs off when they cite their depression as the reason for their behavior.

▶ A person's partner does not leave them while they are depressed or suicidal.

▶ An individual is afraid of letting people get close to them. They act outlandishly, and people withdraw from them.

▶ A person with social anxiety feels understood when

they start learning about social anxiety. They create an identity around having anxiety.

▸ A client finds the pressure of their work and/or achieving overwhelming. If they get "unsick" they will need to return to work and fulfill their own or others' high expectations. The benefits of staying sick (this could be chronic fatigue, an eating disorder, etc.) are reinforced.

▸ Someone is afraid of succeeding almost as much as they are afraid of failing. This person knows that making changes to their work process would give them a chance of succeeding on a much bigger scale than their current level of success. They don't make the changes they know are likely to help, because when they get started on the changes, they get a spike in anxiety about succeeding.

▸ An individual "puts off" certain aspects of their life, such as dating, until they lose weight. If dating is anxiety-provoking, then the behavior of not losing weight is reinforced.[5]

Secondary gain behavior is real. Sadly, as the preceding examples illustrate, the trade-off between the full pursuit of healing and staying stuck can sometimes fall in favor of what's most comfortable. This includes social, psychological, and other benefits, of which the person himself or herself may not even be aware.

So was there any secondary gain, conscious or subconscious benefit, surrounding my OCD, panic attacks, and agoraphobia? Possibly. As an introvert, I could use the inability to scoot around town as an excuse for not spending time with church members at their homes or even at off-site church-related events. Another potential secondary gain was looking like such a devoted husband that I wanted to include my wife and children in as many of my personal and professional activities as possible. More recently, I wouldn't have to explain what had happened in Seattle.

I don't want to beat myself up over what may or may not have been evidence of secondary gain behavior. At this point I really have no way of accurately assessing what was going on in that area. I *can* say with certainty, however, that the vast amount of mental energy devoted to battling the shame and embarrassment of not living up to others' perceived expectations far outweighed any advantages that may have accompanied secondary gain.

That spring, still residing in Michigan, I completed my latest book. Feeling that my writing was at least tangentially attached to my core area of interest—spirituality— helped to fend off the nagging sense that I was doomed to a life devoted to a less-than-fulfilling occupation. The inability to drive any distance alone continued to complicate all aspects of my life.

But one day something happened at the furniture store that set in motion a series of events that I can still hardly wrap my mind around. No, it didn't involve Lonnie Ali or the arrival of the first berber carpet in our warehouse (the same warehouse in which I managed to drive the twelve-foot carpet boom through the wall and into the showroom, but that is for a different book).

"Randy, there's a phone call for you," Pat, the company co-owner, called across the showroom floor. I paused from shuffling papers in my little cubbyhole office and lifted the extension phone handset.

"This is Jeannette Johnson with *Guide* magazine," came the voice on the other end of the line. I knew about *Guide*, a weekly Christian magazine for kids ages 10-14. In fact, I'd received it at church when I was that age, though I'd seldom read it. Not that it was a poorly done magazine, but I simply wasn't a reader.

After exchanging pleasantries, Jeannette continued. "Randy, this is going to sound a little strange, but let me share something with you."

"Sure," I responded.

"Our assistant editor is leaving, and I was praying about who might fill that spot. Well, right there in the middle of my prayer, I seemed to get the impression, *Call Raina Osborne*."

Raina was a mutual acquaintance and had been a magazine editor before following other pursuits.

"So I did that, and when I asked her if she could think of someone who might make a good assistant editor for our magazine, she immediately gave me your name." She continued, and eventually asked if I'd be interested in submitting a résumé. "Oh, and by the way, I'll be in your area in a couple of weeks. I'd love to meet you in person." The whole thing blindsided me, but I told her I'd get a résumé sent off to her.

A couple of weeks later, I strolled into the main library on the university campus, where Jeannette and I had agreed to meet. I quickly recognized her from the editorial photo that appeared in the magazine. After exchanging pleasantries and discussing the position, I knew what I had to do. Committed to not putting another employer in a bad position such as I'd done in Seattle, it was time for some straight talk about my condition.

"Jeannette, I need to tell you about something I'm dealing with," I began. She listened intently as I shared my struggle with agoraphobia and the accompanying travel challenges. Since *Guide* is a national publication, with even some overseas subscribers, I wasn't sure how this tale of woe would sit with my potential boss. Surely it was not out of the question that such dysfunction could be a deal-breaker.

As hard as I tried to prevent it, a dam broke. The emotions of the past few months resulted in tears beginning to slide down my cheeks. *This is just great,* I thought. *Just what every employer wants to see in a new employee—an inability to control their own emotions. And during the first interview! How much worse an impression could I possibly make?*

At last I brought my story to a close. After a moment of thoughtful silence, Jeannette spoke. "Randy, one thing I've learned through the years," she said, "is that a person's pain makes you that much more sensitive to others' struggles." Then she smiled and added, "I don't see a problem here."

Had I heard correctly? After everything I'd just told her, she "didn't see a problem"? She was willing to give me a shot as part of a magazine staff despite my immense behavioral baggage?

A few weeks later, we drove to Maryland, where I met the rest of the staff and the company president. It soon became clear that Jeannette intended to recommend that I start with the magazine as soon as possible. The facility, including editorial offices and printing plant, was located on 133 beautiful rolling acres in western Maryland. I could hardly believe my good fortune. It seemed there was a God after all!

I loved my new job. My proclivity for thinking like a kid was suddenly helping to pay the rent. Days were filled with brainstorming creative titles, coming up with new ways to address old topics, working with authors, and even tossing in a short editorial of my own every other week. Jeannette patiently mentored me, expressing ample appreciation for my efforts along the way, no matter how wacky some of them undoubtedly seemed to her.

With Jeannette's approval, sometimes I practiced driving alone during work hours. Over time I was able to move well past the city limits, though never without some degree of anxious discomfort. When I finally reached Frederick, the next closest city, I celebrated with a root beer float at a local diner there. Still, I was slugging it out, and more than once I wondered if it was really worth it. Was I making progress? You bet. Was a breakthrough at hand? Not by a long shot. I was still just dabbling around the edges of a much larger picture.

One Sunday morning the sun shone bright and warm through our south-facing bedroom window. I'd slept in, and as I slowly awoke, a sense of peace bordering on bliss washed over me. I basked in the powerful aura—a welcome but unfamiliar sensation that evoked a palpable reaction. A smile crossed my face, and for once everything seemed perfect. It was as if someone had pulled the plug on all my anxieties. Everything about my life had suddenly found its center. The peace was so rapturous that its memory has never faded.

This state of nirvana lasted for perhaps fifteen seconds. Then my mind began "scanning" for trouble. Dr. Baker had once painted a memorable word picture of how "free-floating anxiety" works. "It's as if there are random anxieties floating around in your head," he explained, "and your conscious mind sends out a search party to find them."

Another way to think of this brand of anxiety is like a cattle roundup. The anxiety is on the loose, and the victim's "cowboy" mind acts as a lasso to bring all the stray vexation back into the mind-corral.

That morning it didn't take long for my troubled mind to quash my joy. My serenity quickly succumbed to anxiety, guilt, and shame. Disappointment and resignation washed over me, and the joyous moments passed. Oh, how I longed for such peace to return!

Early on, our editorial division gathered for one of its regular meetings. As we sat around a conference table waiting for the meeting to begin, one person shared their latest promotional gimmick for their particular publication. It was a high-tech version of a mood ring. In this case, it was a little spot on a plastic business card that turned colors depending on your stress level.

"Check this out," John said. "You just touch this area for a few seconds and it will tell if you're relaxed or tense." John passed the card around and everyone had a good laugh.

"Here, Randy," John said, handing the card to me. "Let's see what kind of mood you're in today."

Reluctantly, I pressed my finger down on the magic spot. I could have predicted the results.

"Whoa, check this out!" John announced. "Dude, this thing turned totally black! You must be *really* stressed out!"

Yeah, that was pretty much the story of my life, told right there on a little plastic giveaway.

My editorial colleagues' eyes bugged out at the results this new kid on the block had just provided. Past and present, I'd been viewed as funny and easygoing. Add to that a growing sense of wonder at my relaxed jazz piano playing style, and "uptight" was hard for anyone to associate with my general outward persona.

It's amazing how humans adapt and compensate for their own shortcomings and discomfort. For example, I'd probably agree with most observers that I have some natural talent in several areas, including music, cartooning, writing, and even leadership. In junior high, I was the class clown, which simply meant that I gained attention through shenanigans rather than respectable grades.

Musically, I'd had eight years of formal piano training, yet very little had stuck with me. Instead, I started playing pop tunes by ear, in one or two keys only. But did you know that most popular tunes can be played using very few root chords? I built a large repertoire using this method, and have a vast wedding reception résumé to vouch for my success. (There are even publishers who sell music "fakebooks" aimed at customers like me.) As long as nobody asked me to read a sheet of music, or to play the tune exactly the way it sounded on the radio, I could fake it.

This may have been evidence of a deeper-seated sense that somehow I was "faking it" in life. Dr. Baker, my early therapist, had done his best to correct this kind of faulty thinking. It was ironic that I had published three books before he'd gotten his first work published, a fact we once shared a good laugh about. Still, I longed to be an "expert' in something. If only I could claim that I knew a lot about a subject, then I'd know for sure that I was no longer faking it.

It turns out that in the matter of feeling like a fake, I did not have a corner on the market. There's even a name for this type of thinking: imposter syndrome.

> Impostor syndrome (also known as impostor phenomenon or fraud syndrome) is a term coined in 1978 by clinical psychologists Dr. Pauline R. Clance and Suzanne A. Imes referring to high-achieving individuals marked by an inability to internalize their accomplishments and a persistent fear of being exposed as a 'fraud.' Despite external evidence of their competence, those exhibiting the syndrome remain convinced that they are frauds and do not deserve the success they have achieved. Proof of success is dismissed as luck, timing, or as a result of deceiving others into thinking they are more intelligent and competent than they believe themselves to be.[6]

It took a long time for me to deal an uppercut to this mentality. Sometimes it still haunts me. It's true that there's a lot I can't do and probably even more that I know nothing about. But now I remind myself that while I may not be a world-renowned expert in anything, I do possess some unique gifts, talents, and abilities. Occasionally, I have to remind myself of this fact, and it helps keep things in perspective. After all, is a home-schooling mom a failure because she can't figure out the stock market? Does a nuclear scientist hang his head in shame because he is unable to change the oil in his car? Should certain Mennonites in my community withdraw from the human race because they didn't attend high school?

It's really all about playing well the hand we've been dealt, isn't it? I've tried to do that for quite a while now, and I've accepted the reality that none of us can be all things to all people, including ourselves. The joy—and gift—is in discovering and growing into the person we know we're called to be. For me, that involves dropping the façade, revealing my deeper self, and praying—literally and figuratively—that by moving in this direction someone else might be prompted to more fully embrace their own unique self.

If only I'd understood during the worst of my journey what I know now, my recovery journey might have been at least a bit accelerated. As it was, I still had much to learn.

"Randy, this is Bill." My former seminary pal and I had stayed in touch through the few years. Bill had successfully pastored a couple of churches, but his personal life was a different story. Now his marriage had fallen irreparably apart, and a fierce custody battle between he and his wife was taking place over their two boys.

"Oh, man, Bill, I am so sorry to hear about this," I said after hearing about the latest skirmish. "I wish I could do something."

"Well, Randy, that's why I'm calling. There *is* something you can do."

"Tell me more," I responded.

[*208*]

"I need a 'scribe,'" Bill explained. "You know I can only type with my index fingers, and that's not going work for what has to be done. My lawyer says I need to document everything I can think of regarding why I should gain custody of the boys. You know, incidents showing how the boys and I have been mistreated. I need to build a strong case showing why I deserve to have custody. It's not going to be easy, but with this documentation I may have a shot."

Bill's voice was laced with desperation. He continued speaking.

"Randy, I need to fly you down here so you can be my scribe. I've got all the evidence, but it would take me weeks and weeks to type everything up. I don't have that much time! If you'll just come down here for a weekend, I'll tell you everything and you can type it up for me. You're a writer, Randy! Can you come down to Georgia and do this for me?"

How could I possibly say no to this plea? How could I let down my best friend when he needed exactly what I could offer? My mind swirled, and I shifted uncomfortably in my seat. This wouldn't be the first time I'd crafted a feeble excuse for not being able to perform a task, but it would be one of the most painful—for both of us.

"Wow, Bill, I really wish I could help you out, but, well, we've just moved here and, you know, with a one-and-a-half year-old, well, Diana gets pretty worn out—"

"But it would just be for a weekend!" Bill interrupted. "I know how fast you can type, and I know we could get this done! It could mean the difference between who ends up with the boys!"

I paused for a moment, then went on with some

now-forgotten finish to my excuse-making. There was a palpable sense of disappointment in Bill's voice, but we hung up as friends.

The demons called Frustration, Shame, and Guilt were dressed in their finest that evening. After all, it *was* quite an occasion for them to celebrate. Anxiety had managed to provoke an almost despicable act, one that might have lifelong consequences for two little boys and their family. How could I have done such a thing?

Today, thanks to an increased understanding of the depth of dysfunction I'd been experiencing during that time, I'm a little softer on myself when it comes to that particular incident. What seemed "almost despicable" then, I would now label as "regrettable." I regret that I could not rise to the occasion when my best friend needed me so badly. But now I understand that distressed emotions and imbalanced biochemicals do not constitute moral failure—it just feels that way sometimes.

Bill lost the custody battle. Later, he told me that it would've been a tough sell no matter what. The courts in that particular state tend to side with the mother, sometimes even in the face of clear evidence that she may be less than ideally suited for parenting. That news assuaged a bit of my distress at not having supported my friend, but Frustration, Shame, and Guilt were not about to call it quits. They'd show up to celebrate another victory many more times.

A few months into my new editorial role, the first travel challenge came along. Our team was slated to make a showing at a huge weeklong youth event in Colorado. After all, our young readers needed to meet the people behind their beloved weekly denominational magazine.

I began to panic about my panic which, as I mentioned earlier, is really a better definition of agoraphobia than the one found in most dictionaries. The latter usually revolves around a fear of open spaces. As a reminder, both fears play a role, but it's the fear of recurring panic symptoms that tends to snowball into mental distress.

"You know, I think maybe I should stay here," I cautiously told Jeannette. "I mean, we *are* a weekly magazine, and there should probably be at least one editor in the building at all times." After a few more excuses, my senior editor either gave in or gave up, likely seeing through my excuse-making and once again demonstrating the beauty of grace. In the end, our graphic designer filled my slot, boarding the plane for Denver while I hung my head in shame yet another time.

For nearly ten more years, I managed to avoid traveling any distance alone. During this time I excelled in my core editorial functions, yet also declined a range of opportunities to expand my professional reach because of my problem with travel. Not that fear of travel is unusual, especially flying. According to a *New York Times* article:

> "Several studies have found that up to 40 percent of people have some degree of anxiety about flying," said Dr. Lucas van Gerwen, an aviation psychologist and professional pilot in the Netherlands and an organizer of an international fear-of-flying conference, sponsored by the International Civil Aviation Organization. . . .

> According to the National Institute of Mental

Health, the percentage of Americans who have a fear of flying so intense that it qualifies as a phobia or anxiety disorder and keeps them off airplanes is closer to 6.5 percent.[7]

Still, most of those same people can drive down the highway alone in an automobile for very long distances. Despite my best efforts, I was still stuck in neutral and sometimes feeling as if I might be rolling backward.

FIFTEEN

PASSED BY

Three years into my tenure with the publishing company, my title changed from assistant to associate editor. I left the building each day looking forward to the next with great anticipation. My anxiety still rose to fever pitch on occasion, but by and large I was settling into a workable situation. The occasional call to travel was deftly swatted away, and my colleagues and supervisors apparently weren't calling into question my apparent lack of interest in hitting the road, or the skies. Either my proven skills were assuaging any concerns along these lines, or my senior editor was covering for me. Maybe it was a little of both, but somehow, I was not only surviving but thriving in this creative magazine publishing environment.

By now we had three children, all boys, and Diana had chosen to home-school them for at least a while. Home-schooling families are notorious for "on-hands" adventures such as field trips and other such learning experiences. When the distance to be traveled exceeded the city limits, I began shifting nervously in my editorial chair. No, I wasn't the one driving off, but my "safe person" would be out of reach, just as when I'd trailed Diana into downtown Seattle.

The mind-body connection is a beautiful thing—except when the circuits misfire. Somehow, my brain still processed the unavailability of a "safe" person as a crisis. How did that happen in the first place? Dr. Baker and others might trace it back to "unempathic bonding" between mother and child, that whole "separation anxiety" thing. I suspect this theory harbors at least some degree of truth. But I've also come to believe that anxiety disorders can hardly be pinned on imperfect mothering alone. What about Dad? How about genes? Who knows? Maybe even growing up directly across from an orchard constantly bombarded with insecticide played a role! It takes a long list of ingredients to bake a perfect cake of mental misery.

One morning Jeannette walked into my office and made an announcement. "Well, Randy, I've accepted another job." She explained how she'd grown restless at the magazine, and now she'd be working for an international relief agency traveling the globe and sending back reports for fundraising and other purposes. Then she smiled, pointed to her own workspace, and said, "It's time for you to occupy that chair."

Me? Senior editor? Sure, I could handle the daily responsibilities with no problem. But what about the travel?

Sure enough, Jeannette recommended me for the position of senior editor.

The president invited me over to his lovely home to discuss the editorial opening. After some pleasantries, he got right to the point. "I'm ready to recommend your name to the board," he said with a smile.

I began to panic. My heart pounded, and my palms grew sweaty. I used my diminishing breath to form my next few sentences. "Well, I'm honored, but you see— well, I've got three kids at home, and I really don't want to be one of those dads who's never around," I explained to the president.

The man lifted an eyebrow and looked sideways at me. The cherished position of *Guide* senior editor usually came open only every decade or so, and he was struggling with my reasoning. "Why not take the family along with you?" he pressed. "That's what I used to do back in the day." He was referring to his earlier years in the publishing industry.

"Well, um, I'm not sure that would work out," I mumbled. I wasn't about to lug my family around the country—and possibly internationally—just because their husband and father couldn't travel alone.

"So you really don't want to be considered?" he asked at last.

"Um, well, probably not this time," I replied with an undoubtedly noticeable lack of conviction. I left his home struggling more than ever to rationalize in my own mind that this was the right decision. But deep down, I knew that I could chalk up another failure.

As a gesture of confidence in my abilities, I was essentially given the opportunity to select my new boss. The candidate I recommended was Carolyn, an excellent writer who was currently teaching junior high school in the Pacific Northwest. In interviewing my potential supervisor (how weird is that?), I could tell that she was a great person. There was just one problem: she had just started the school year and was bound to her contract. Carolyn politely thanked me for the opportunity to be considered but said that it didn't seem as if it would work out timing-wise.

Something about Carolyn caused me to not give up easily. A couple of weeks later, I called her back, just to be sure. I even sweetened the deal.

"Carolyn, would you consider taking this position if I shouldered the editorial responsibilities alone until the end of the school year?"

There was a prolonged silence on the other end of the line. Finally, Carolyn sighed, then spoke slowly, as if she were experiencing some form of mild distress. "Well, I guess that's that," she said quietly. "Randy, I've prayed about this over the past couple of weeks. I told the Lord that if the offer came again and you said you were willing to wait until the end of the school year, I'd accept."

I felt sort of awful, and yet I was a little bit thrilled. This seemed like nothing short of unmitigated divine intervention, which could only mean good things for the staff and our publication.

Carolyn's editorship was outstanding—and short-lived. The power of romance was strong, and about a year later the woman—still a close friend to this day—confided to me that when she came to Maryland she'd left a love interest behind in Oregon. Absence had done nothing but make their hearts grow fonder, and Carolyn was giving me the head's-up that marriage was probably soon forthcoming. She also made it clear that her fiancée would not be moving to Maryland, so I'd better start planning for another editorial transition.

By this time, I very much wanted to become senior editor of our publication. Yes, I was tired of counting things, clicking my teeth, and not being able to travel alone. But I was more tired of seeing my dreams crushed at every turn. Unfortunately, bottomless frustration is not much of an elixir, and once again I found myself struggling to envision myself accepting the position should it again be offered to me.

One day I got the call—the new president wanted to see me in his office. After the customary small talk, he refocused the conversation. "Randy, you probably know why I called. Carolyn will be leaving soon, and I'd like to recommend your name to the board to assume the magazine's senior editorship. Are you ready to step into that role?"

Although I considered our new president a friend, I'd never shared anything with him about my challenges. Rather than blurting out "I can't travel anywhere alone!" I gently approached the subject.

"Well, I, um, think I could handle the job, but, uh, what kind of travel would be required?"

"Oh, not all that much, I suppose. Just the usual—a convention once in a while, that kind of thing."

"Not all that much" was a whole lot more than I could do at present. Still, maybe there was some hope.

"I'm going to be up front with you about something," I said. "You see, well, I've got a little issue with travel. I get sort of uncomfortable when I have to go to certain places."

"Well, we all have different comfort zones," he responded. "But it's good to get out once in a while; it gives you new perspectives." He paused, smiled, and pointed out his second-floor corner office window. "Now, if you couldn't even drive to the top of South Mountain over there, well, that might be a problem." The man smiled as he lowered his hand. He clearly had no idea of my situation.

I was silent for a moment, struggling to find just the right words that might somehow keep the door of opportunity from slamming shut in my face. At last I said, "I think travel is going to be a problem for me. So, well, I guess I'll need to decline this time around."

It turned out there would be no further discussion or accommodation for my situation. A few days later my vice president stopped by my office. "Randy, I just came from the Administrative Committee meeting. I thought I should let you know that we voted for Tim to become the next editor." Tim was the assistant editor for another publication, and his office was down just a few doors from mine.

I let out a sigh. "I see."

My vice president continued. "Man, I'm sorry it didn't work out for you. Someone mentioned something about some kind of travel issue. I'm not sure what that was all about, but in the end we all agreed that the new editor would need to be able to travel. I'm really sorry, Randy."

Secretly, I'd been hoping administration would find a workaround for me, but no luck. Tim was a good friend with less magazine editorial experience than I had, but now he'd be my boss.

About a week later, I happened to be at an event held at Tim's church. "So you turned 'em down again, huh, Randy?" a mutual friend called out with a smile. As luck would have it, Tim's wife happened to be standing nearby. The same mutual friend turned toward her and said, "I heard your husband accepted the position."

The woman smiled awkwardly and finally said, "Yes, he's excited about it. He likes a challenge."

I casually sauntered away, once again despair threatening to overwhelm me.

As it turned out, Tim's term of service was even shorter than Carolyn's. His former company wooed him back home just about a year later, once again leaving me viewed as the logical person to step into the position. After all, I'd been on staff for over a decade, for pity's sake. Wasn't it about time to take the leap?

Even though I'd practiced a lot, I still couldn't drive more than a few miles without experiencing panic symptoms. Sure, that was more than the three blocks of a decade earlier, but hardly a breakthrough.

In 1960, Elvis Presley scored big with the ballad "It's Now or Never." Though I was never a big Elvis fan, I shared the sentiment reflected in this song. Somehow, I knew the time had come to take a risk—it really was now or never.

SIXTEEN

"I THINK I CAN HELP YOU"

In 1970, Dr. Julius Axelrod, the son of Polish immigrants, received the Nobel Prize in physiology or medicine. Hard work and sheer brilliance enabled Axelrod to climb the academic ladder and land various coveted research positions.

During the 1960s, Axelrod was working at the National Institutes of Health in Bethesda, Maryland. Having earlier lost his left eye in a laboratory accident, the Jewish researcher refused to let such a small thing deter his scientific efforts. Intrigued by the role that chemical messengers known as neurotransmitters play in the brain, he began focusing his research in that area.

"Neurotransmitters are hormones that are stored in nerve endings or terminals located in the brain. When neurotransmitters are released from nerve endings, they cross the synapse (the space between nerves) and send chemical messages from the brain across nerve channels. Receptor molecules in the post-synaptic (receiving) nerve endings recognize pre-synaptic (sending) neurotransmitters. These receptors are specially shaped to receive the appropriate neurotransmitters, which fit in the receptor like a key in a lock. Epinephrine (also known as adrenaline) and its chemical cousin, norepinephrine (also called noradrenaline), are members of a class of hormones called the catecholamines, which function as neurotransmitters in the sympathetic nervous system."[1]

A key finding revealed that neurotransmitters are not a one-time messenger. Using an instrument known as a spectrophotofluorometer, or SPF, Axelrod "was able to measure tiny amounts of neurotransmitters in the brain. He studied norepinephrine and described the process for storage, release, and "re-uptake" by the cells as needed."[2] In other words, neurotransmitters are not a "once and done" entity; they do their job over and over. At least, that's the way it's *supposed* to work.

When the laboratory dust had settled, Axelrod's research would pave the way for a new avenue of hope for people like me—selective serotonin reuptake inhibitors, or SSRIs. These drugs "ease depression by increasing levels of serotonin in the brain. Serotonin is one of the chemical messengers (neurotransmitters) that carry signals between brain cells. SSRIs block the reabsorption (reuptake) of serotonin in the brain, making more serotonin available. SSRIs are called selective because they seem to primarily affect serotonin, not other neurotransmitters."[3]

But, just as the above description from MayoClinic.org indicates, my understanding was that SSRIs were for people with depression. I wasn't depressed, at least, not any more than the next person, or so I reasoned. No, my struggled revolved around anxiety and obsessive behavior and anxiety. I was not yet aware that "SSRIs also may be used to treat conditions other than depression, such as anxiety disorders."[4]

Only later would I begin to see the complex interplay between all of these disorders.

These new medications hit the market in fits and starts. "The first successful launch was of a compound called fluvoxamine, which has the trade names Faverin® and Luvox®. But the next launch was more significant. Eli Lilley launched fluoxetine in 1987 . . . under its trade name of Prozac®." Still another, paroxetine, hit the market in the United Kingdom under the name Serotax®. In 1993, it became available under the trade name Paxil®.[5]

A falling star. A classic car. A beautiful woman, or a man with handsome chiseled features. Different things catch peoples' eyes. I suppose it all has something to do with what's been taking up space in a person's head.

One afternoon I took a shortcut through our company library. Glancing down at a cart containing books about to be reshelved, one title caught my eye: *You Mean I Don't Have to Feel This Way?* But the subtitle is what caused me to give it a closer look: "New Help for Anxiety, Depression, and Addiction." The book didn't get reshelved right then, because I took it from the cart, signed my name on the card, and tossed it in the self-checkout box.

At home I began reading how the author, Colette Dowling, and her daughter had been in Europe when the latter experienced her first panic attack. I was riveted not only by the writing but because I identified so deeply with everything taking place in the book. Toward the end, Dowling included a good overview of the then-new SSRI medications, and the dramatic difference they'd made to not only her daughter but to so many others.

Wait a minute, I thought. *Is it possible that* I *really* don't *have to feel this way?* Beyond that, I wondered if it was more than coincidence that I'd stumbled across this book. Could the convergence of my disorder, new medications, and this very book be signaling to me that it was time to take action?

It was perhaps the most difficult phone call I'd ever made. After all, it's not with great enthusiasm that one books an appointment with a psychiatrist. But by now, after all the years of frustration and disappointment, I could feel an ample dose of depression enveloping me. I sensed that if my personal and professional circumstances were to change, I'd need to muster my courage and take a risk.

A couple of weeks later I found myself in the office of Dr. Matthew Wagner, who'd reserved a one-hour time slot for me. It didn't take him long to verify my foremost symptoms as agoraphobia. Panic disorder and obsessive-compulsive disorder completed the three-piece set, but they didn't affect my daily functioning as much as agoraphobia.

Dr. Wagner listened with great compassion to my story. I shared with him my deep resistance to taking medication, and how I'd heard that pills were nothing but a "crutch" for people who couldn't deal with the real issues. I also explained that I'd finally arrived at a place where I knew that I had to explore every possible avenue of hope and healing. "And," I concluded, "I read that there's some new kind of medication that might be worth trying."

After I finished, he took in a deep breath, looked me in the eyes, and uttered six simple but game-and-life-changing words: "I think I can help you." The surge of hope that shot through my system at hearing those words was unforgettable.

Dr. Wagner continued. "Randy, above everything else, I see my job as helping others to find relief from suffering. If a medication helps that to happen, I believe it's a good thing."

Until that moment, I'd reasoned that anything short of total healing was unacceptable. For the first time, it occurred to me that perhaps the easing of suffering was a worthy goal in and of itself.

When I told Dr. Wagner that I simply could not envision ever traveling alone for long distances, he had an encouraging response for that as well. "I wouldn't underestimate the possibilities for progress," he said. "It may not happen overnight, but once you begin doing the things you used to do and going places where you used to go, you may be surprised at how the pieces begin falling back into place."

Something was stirring deep inside me. Was any of this really possible?

"After all these years, it almost sounds too good to be true," I admitted. "But maybe one of those new medications—I've heard about one called Prozac®—can help me turn the corner."

"Well, Prozac® *is* in the class of medications called SS-RIs," Dr. Wagner said, "but that's not the one I'm thinking is best for your situation. There's another one called Paxil® that I think you might want to try." He went on to explain the benefits—and side effects—associated with this pill I knew nothing about.

[225]

"But I've got another question," I said. "Um, will the medication, like, change my personality or anything? I mean, in general, I still pretty much like who I am," I added with a smile.

Dr. Wagner smiled back. "No, Randy, you won't become someone else. In fact, you'll become *more* like the real you than you've been in a long time."

I liked that idea.

"So what do you think?" asked Dr. Wagner. "Would you like to go ahead with the medication?"

After a pause, I said, "Yes, I think I should give it a try."

As we neared the end of our session, Dr. Wagner told me that it would be a very good idea to work with a counselor for a while. "Spending time bringing some issues to the surface is always going to be better than just taking a medication alone," he explained. He gave me the name of a counselor in whom he had confidence, and I left his office with the prescription in hand.

But I didn't head to the pharmacy. Instead, I placed the prescription in the cupboard above our refrigerator. Resistance to putting something potentially "mind-altering" into my system still ran deep. Besides, so long as the prescription remained unfilled, I still had hope that it would change my life once I actually did take it. If, on the other hand, I took the medication and it solved nothing, I'd be left without hope.

Days turned into weeks, and still the unfilled prescription remained in the cupboard.

During this time my church was hosting a satellite TV preaching series. We'd invited our entire community to watch the meetings at our church, which were being simultaneously broadcast to over seventy countries.

In an effort to maintain her sanity by occasionally escaping home school duties and parenting three boys, Diana had taken a part-time job at a nearby local bookstore. Tonight, she was working at the store. That left me to haul our two older boys to our church's Adventurer Club meeting, something akin to Cub Scouts. Since I'd not been able to attend the satellite series, I figured rather than go all the way home, I'd take the older boys to their meeting and slip into the church sanctuary with our youngest son and watch the televised event.

Ethan and I slid into a pew near the back of the church and focused on the preacher now appearing on the huge screen. His sermon was tight, and he delivered it with energy. Still, after a long day at work, I wasn't completely enthralled.

That was about to change.

I am not making up what happened next. As the featured speaker began wrapping up his presentation, he bore down with an illustration. "There was a very sick man," he began. "But he didn't have to stay that way, because next to his bed, on a shelf, was a bottle of medicine that would save his life."

My ears perked up.

The speaker continued. "Now, here's what nobody could understand: the man refused to simply reach over and take the medicine!"

The hairs on the back of my neck began to stand on end.

"Yes, that's right! The solution to his problem was just an arm's length away, but he refused to do anything about it!"

I glanced around, wondering if anyone else in the church or around the globe knew that this preacher was talking about me. Of course, the "medicine" in his illustration was the gospel, but I knew there were other kinds of medicine that people refused to take—and prescriptions that people refused to get filled.

"Friends, your life can be different, but *you must reach over and take the medicine.*" With that, the speaker concluded his message, and I tried to regain my composure.

What had just happened? Had God Himself in some mystical way just spoken directly to me through this satellite presentation? While some would call it a coincidence—and maybe it was—I have chosen to believe otherwise. That night as I drove home I could not shake the sense that something very personal and other-worldly had just taken place.

Still, it took another nudge to get me to actually make a trip to the pharmacy with the prescription in hand.

"You mean to tell me that you've got a prescription but you haven't had it filled yet?" my former seminary buddy, Bill, asked in astonishment over the phone.

"Yeah, well, you know, I just don't know what it'll do to me," I sheepishly admitted.

"I'll tell you what it will do to you," Bill said, a scolding tone evident in his voice. "It'll help you get your life back. Randy, you *must* take that medication!"

"Yeah, I know," I responded softly.

After his painful divorce, Bill had now married a physician, and Alicia knew something about SSRIs. "It seems that these types of medications kind of balance out brain chemistry," Alicia explained. "It might provide just what your particular brain chemistry needs."

Alicia shared some more details about the medication, then put Bill back on the phone. "I'm going to make you a deal, Randy. How would you like to take a trip to visit us down here in Florida?"

"Of course, I'd love to do that, but—"

Bill cut me off. "OK, then, here's the deal. You take that medication. When you're ready to come and visit us, we'll pay for your airfare. What do you say?"

I took in a deep breath, and finally said, "Deal." I meant what I said, and a short while later found me beginning the medication regime that Dr. Wagner had prescribed. The target was to get me on a 40 mg. daily dose, then take it either up or down from there, depending on what seemed to be most effective.

It took about a week before I knew something was changing with my brain's chemistry. While undoubtedly psychoactive medications affect people differently, my recollection of what occurred is quite distinct. I awoke rather abruptly about 3 A.M. With my eyes still closed, I began seeing what can only be described as psychedelic patterns. Vibrant colors swirled, then stopped, swirled, then stopped. This pattern repeated itself so long as my eyes were closed. The sensation itself was not unpleasant, yet because it was so unfamiliar to me, I found it disturbing.

I sat up in bed and nudged Diana. "Something's going on," I said. "I think it's the medication." Had something gone terribly wrong, or was this colorful psychic phenomenon simply a part of the process? I had no way of knowing right then, but eventually, I managed to settle back down and fall asleep.

First thing upon awakening, I called Dr. Wagner's office. After explaining what I'd experienced, he suggested that it was probably some kind of "intrapsychic cross-talk." In layperson's terms, I understood this to mean that various portions of my brain were attempting to communicate with one another in brand-new ways. Since Dr. Wagner didn't seem concerned, I decided I wouldn't be either.

The kind of medication I was taking, an SSRI, has received affirmation. For example, the National Alliance on Mental Illness states, "To date, there are no known problems associated with long term use of paroxetine [Paxil®]. It is a safe and effective medication when used as directed."[4]

On the other hand, the Internet is replete with "big pharma" conspiracy websites, along with ample discussion board posts, about the horrors of this evil drug.

The fact is, any medication has side effects, and Paxil® is no exception. Indeed, more recent cautions have been issued regarding its use by children and teens,[5] and it has been associated with some other negative outcomes.[6] Shocking as it may seem, life on Planet Earth comes with risks, some of which appear as warning labels on prescription drugs. But in the United States those labels are preceded by stacks of research studies and eventual approval by the Federal Drug Administration. Is the system imperfect? Yes. For example, Paxil® can be quite uncomfortable to discontinue. That's why every person must weigh the evidence and associated risks and make his or her own decision. I decided the risks paled in comparison to the years of suffering I'd endured.

Over the course of several weeks, the medication took hold. One of the initial unwelcome side effects was drowsiness. As the full 40 mg. dosage reached full efficacy in my bloodstream, I had a hard time staying awake in my office. Thankfully, I could close my door and catch a few zzz's when necessary. But meetings were a different story. I did my best to get as much night-time sleep as possible in the hope that daytime drowsiness might become less an issue. Sometimes, the sleep helped, but other times, people mentioned the half-opened position of my eyelids. But there was little doubt that my anxiety was on a downward trajectory, so I stuck with the program.

Vivid dreams had come and gone for much of my life, but now they were becoming a nightly occurrence. As Dr. Wagner told me, "Lucid dreaming is a common side effect for many people taking these medications."

The trajectory of my dreams tended to parallel my recovery. Almost immediately, I began to see the veracity of certain aspects of renowned psychiatrist Carl Jung's "dream images," or "archetypes." While I don't subscribe to all aspects of Jung's dream theory, the general idea of dream archetypes seems valid.

My primary archetype is not as unusual as I once thought. "Jungian therapy abounds with house symbols, because they are often central to the meaning of dreams," writes psychotherapist and Jungian analyst Brian Collinson. "The house is one of the most common dream symbols. In dreams, the home often symbolizes the dreamer's entire psyche or personality. Is the dream house well-kept, or does it appear neglected? Is it made of solid stuff or shoddy materials, and thus perhaps in need of renovation? Does the house seem well proportioned? Are its internal spaces cramped or spacious?"[6]

At first when on the medication, my lucid dreams invariably included two main themes. First, there were often threats and violence to my well-being. I have been stalked, mugged, and even stabbed in my dreams. These types of dream components tended to abate as healing continued.

The second and more frequent dream theme found me in a house with a leaking roof, unstable floor, crooked walls, or all of the above. According to Jungian dream theory as mentioned above, this meant that my psyche was in need of serious renovation. I believe this is true. At one point I wrote about this in my journal, an entry I titled "My Heart, My Home":

"For years now I have had a 'dream theme' of homes and home-building, mostly remodeling. Usually, the home under construction is my childhood home. It is always being remodeled or fixed in some way, usually inadequately, and usually, I am the one responsible for the poor job.

"But since therapy (the most recent round, and by far the most helpful), I have dreamed about all the other places where I've lived, at least the major ones. Often, I have considered it a tragedy to see my childhood home change, such as when it was totally redone so as to be unrecognizable."

The entry then notes the main themes of these "house dreams":

1. The house is always unsecure, with doors being left unlocked or some way for intruders to enter.

2. The repair work I am responsible for is always inadequate, with floors being shaky, the roof leaking, etc.

3. In the case of my boyhood home, sometimes people

come and park there and then drive off to work in the morning while I am still asleep. *Who are these workers? I wonder.*

4. There is never a sense of solidness to these houses. Sometimes, I even have to take my family away to safety. (One time a flood was on its way!)

My journal entry continues.

"So what is this 'house' that is always being repaired? . . . I believe it represents my very personhood, all the uncertainties and insecurities of a life lived on 'unsolid' ground."

I go on to speak of various entities that may have produced an unstable structure, from genes to imperfect parenting. But eventually, I conclude the following:

Yes, I have some "anxious genes" and maybe even a biochemical imbalance when it comes to anxiety. But now I am ready to move on. I want to build my life with "concrete"—a home of my own making. This "heart-home" must be built slowly and deliberately as I move out of those homes that have been so insecure and into one in which the foundation is my very God-given personhood. The construction of such a solid, new heart-home must take place one block at a time, or so I suspect. And the place where I build may not be "perfect" ground. But I must build my own heart-home, and not move into someone else's structure . . . . I want to go home and live within the secure confines of a heart and life made whole

Over time, I have found these dreams both mystical and helpful. They have served as a kind of barometer of

[*233*]

the healing process. Again, I don't put full stock in the entire spectrum of Jungian dream analysis. In general, I think dreams serve as a mental filing system, a repository for the day's and years' activities. My experience has been that certain "file drawers" are opened depending on my emotional state. Stressful periods still produce anxious dreams, and more peaceful times result in more positive dreams. Most important, the arc of my dream life has shown steady movement toward a more stable structure, and I find this deeply satisfying.

After some months on the medication, the morning had finally come to drive to Dulles International Airport, some sixty-five miles away—alone. I had a plane to catch; Orlando awaited.

I waved goodbye to Diana and pulled out of the driveway, still a little unsure of what to expect. My driving distances had rapidly increased over the past few weeks, but this was different. Instead of turning around and heading for home after a "practice run," I'd be parking in Remote Parking Lot B, boarding a shuttle bus to the airport, and boxing myself into a flying tin can headed for Florida. There would literally be no chance for escape.

But as I entered the on-ramp to Interstate 70, instead of my heart palpitating, it began to sing. I was really doing this! I was a little uneasy, maybe, but certainly not anywhere close to panicking. Then I noticed something I'd not felt in many years: I was beginning to relax behind the steering wheel! I turned up a tune I'd brought along for the occasion. It felt as if I were almost . . . *normal*. This feeling seemed so unfamiliar that I hardly recognized it. The drivers ahead, beside, and behind me, well, most of them had probably been doing this practically in their sleep. If only I could shout my joy to them on this early Friday morning!

At Dulles International Airport I pulled into Remote Parking Lot B as if it were a NASCAR victory lane. Sure, it had been only sixty-five miles, but it had been *more than two decades* since I'd traveled that distance by myself.

Grabbing my bags from the back seat, I awaited the shuttle bus, which pulled up to the main terminal about ten minutes later. When we arrived at our destination, I walked down the bus steps and into the terminal. From all outward appearances, I looked like I'd been doing this on a regular basis. Inwardly, I was still a little uncertain, but nothing could stop me now. Within a couple of hours I was 25,000 feet in the air, headed toward Orlando. Did my fellow passengers have any inkling of the momentous nature of this event? Or was it possible that at least a few of them had also somehow overcome their own fears and phobias enough to make this flight?

The weekend was wonderful, the most disappointing aspect being that I never saw a live alligator, as I'd hoped. But emotionally, the entire experience seemed like a dream whose fulfillment had seemed impossible just months earlier.

Returning home a few days later, I left Dulles and Virginia behind, heading for home in Maryland. What happened along the way caught me totally off-guard: I started slowing down! I suddenly realized that the sooner I got home, the more quickly the incredible and newfound feeling of freedom would fade. No, this must be prolonged, savored! After all, I could drive and travel solo again without panic! A new life had begun—a life that suddenly held promise far beyond my wildest dreams.

Along with the medication, I continued seeing a licensed clinical aocial worker (LCSW), following up on one of the individuals recommended by Dr. Wagner. Chris was a perfect match, and she was instrumental in helping me to dig into some issues I'd neglected to fully deal with earlier in my therapeutic experience. At first we met twice weekly. This early double-dipping was key to maintaining a healing momentum. Eventually, we cut back to one weekly session, and that lasted for a few months.

"Talk therapy" naysayers would do well to reserve judgment regarding the benefits of this treatment modality until they've experienced it for themselves. Although in my particular case I now view medication as the first-tier transformative element in rising above anxiety, the sessions with Chris were crucial. Her skills enabled me not only to discover long-buried unhealthy thought patterns, often rooted in childhood experiences, but to process them in healing ways. One of her goals was to help me recognize cognitive "walls" that had been built in my brain. This was all part of a complex, compartmentalized infrastructure I'd subconsciously built, the end-game being nothing short of mental and emotional survival.

One day, Chris and I were exploring some particular aspect of my childhood (I don't remember the details) when I began weeping. I tried to hold it back, but it was no use. The weeping turned into heaving sobs, and I was utterly unable to stop the torrent. Somehow, I was able to ask Chris to leave the room, which she kindly did. The flood of emotions and tears had continued for about ten minutes, when Chris gently cracked open the door to check on me. "Everything OK?" she asked quietly.

I shook my head no and waved her off. She quietly closed the door, leaving me eventually to drain myself of tears after some twenty minutes. Chris returned at last and sat down across from me. "I think one of those walls we talked about just came down," she said. I nodded, exhausted and relieved, yet still unsure as to what exactly had just happened. All I knew was that my implosion felt healthy in some way. Maybe the next house I dreamed about would be a little sturdier.

Just as I did, many individuals view psychotropic medications as a "crutch" that should be considered only a step toward healing. Even some psychiatrists who affirm the value of medication often view them as a "temporary" fix. Some therapists simply don't want their clients to be on medications on a permanent basis, at least if possible. However, these therapists may encourage clients to at least try medication on a temporary basis. Also, some people *may* be able to "wean" off medication at some point with the guidance of a physician or psychiatrist. But in no case should medication be viewed as reserved for only the "weak."

Again, I am not suggesting that a pill alone should be viewed as the ultimate and lone solution when dealing with anxiety disorders. While Paxil®, worked for me, it may not be right for the next person. Indeed, recently a friend told me about her negative experience with Paxil®, and that she would recommend it to "no one." That's wise on her part, because she is not a medical professional! And while I'm not "recommending" any drug or class of drug for the same reason, neither should their value as a short- or long-term component to ongoing resolution be underestimated.

In a *Huffington Post* blog post, "Why I Chose Anti-anxiety Medication," Elli Thompson Purtell shares her own journey toward recovery. Referring to the difference finding the proper biochemical support made in her life, Purtell writes:

> Ultimately, we agreed to try a low dose of medication—something I had resisted for so long and continued to be wary of. But just one month later, I got my life back. I felt like myself for the first time in years. I always considered myself happy, but I was often too anxious to *enjoy* being happy. On this medication, the cloud was lifted. The continuous loop of worrying thoughts was finally severed. My mind was able to move forward and soak up the wonderful life I had. Four years later, I am still on the same low dose, and I am grateful *every day* for this medication.[7]

In fairness, Purtell says that medication is probably not for everyone, that some forms of anxiety can be overcome without it, and that she hopes "to wean myself off of my medication one day soon."[8] But she adds:

"I also know that some anxiety is truly crippling. It makes you a prisoner to your own mind. It exhaustively beats your spirit to a pulp. It doesn't go away no matter what you try and how badly you want to change.

> I cannot stress enough how important it is that everyone, especially those who don't suffer from

anxiety, refrain from judgment and understand that this is a real disease that is often beyond one's control. So-called experts and the average Joe alike have opinions about the ultimate solution to anxiety (and a host of other conditions), but there is no one-size-fits-all answer. The right remedy varies from person to person.[9]

I couldn't have said it better myself, although I'm writing an entire book in the hope of doing just that.

So what about it? Are anxiety disorders just a figment of a dysfunctional imagination, or is something more going on? Do SSRIs, SNRIs, and other medications actually work, or are they simply expensive placebos?

First, it's important to recognize that it's actually not totally understood how serotonin medications work. A further brief look at the mechanisms behind SSRIs is important. As already mentioned, the general consensus goes as follows: "It's thought that SSRIs work by increasing serotonin levels in the brain. Serotonin is a neurotransmitter (a messenger chemical that carries signals between nerve cells in the brain). It's thought to have a good influence on mood, emotion, and sleep. After carrying a message, serotonin is usually reabsorbed by the nerve cells (known as "reuptake"). SSRIs work by blocking ("inhibiting") reuptake, meaning more serotonin is available to pass further messages between nearby nerve cells."[10]

However, "It would be too simplistic to say that depression and related mental health conditions are caused by low serotonin levels, but a rise in serotonin levels can improve symptoms and make people more responsive to other types of treatment."[11]

The answer to so much surrounding the relationship between anxiety disorders and medication is an unequivocal yes, no, always, and never. The human brain remains a vast mystery. I would be remiss in forcefully stating that Paxil®, for instance, unquestionably fixed a biochemical imbalance in my brain, the proof of which is found in a life saved from despair and regained ability to travel freely. No, I cannot say that I *know* beyond the shadow of a doubt that this is what happened. But that's the story I'm going with until proven otherwise.

Why am I sticking with it? I call it the "W.O.E. Principle." This simple little acronym stands for "weight of evidence." In my own case, and the case of others such as Elli Purtell, something dramatic and wonderful happened that changed everything. While our progress could be attributed to the placebo effect, which is real indeed, I think something even more powerful, more biophysical, took place.

Beyond my personal experience and opinion, and as I've previously mentioned, there does seem to be increasing evidence of biological factors being involved in anxiety disorders. For example:

A study has linked panic disorder to a wayward hormone in a brain circuit that regulates vigilance. While too little of the hormone, called orexin, is known to underlie narcolepsy, the new study suggests that too much of it may lead to panic attacks that afflict 6 million American adults.[12]

Also, the Brain and Behavior Research Foundation reported:

The unexpected outcome of research by
NARSAD grantee John A. Wemmie, M.D., Ph.D.,
neuroscientist, University of Iowa and his colleagues,
has implications for the future study and treatment
of people with panic disorders. Dr. Wemmie, senior
author for the study published in the latest issue of
Nature Neuroscience, and his team studied subjects
with malfunctioning amygdalas—a fear-processing
center of the brain.[13]

Even if you know nothing about the brain—or think
you know nothing—you are nevertheless quite
aware of your amygdala," writes Barbara Strauch,
deputy science editor and health and medical science
editor at the *New York Times*. "This is your body's
Homeland Security Department. If you see a scary-
looking fellow plane passenger, have to talk with
your boss about your performance, even speak with
your teenager about sex, it's your amygdala that
goes into action, revving up the rest of the body to
make that crucial call: fight or flight?[14]

Between the amygdalae and basal ganglia, there's a lot
of anxious activity taking place.
Back to Wemmie's research:

The study participants were unable to experience
fear when confronted with triggers ranging from
insects to violence due to damage in their amygdalas.
However, despite the abnormal functioning of their
amygdalas, two of the study participants reported
feelings of panic and one had a panic attack

following an experiment in which they temporarily experienced the sensation of suffocation. Such strong reactions to the trigger are common in people with panic disorders.

This finding supports an earlier hypothesis by Antonio Damasio, University of Southern California and his team, which suggests that normal amygdala function is key to processing external threats, but another brain path processes fears related to bodily function. The findings also suggest that malfunctioning of the amygdala may play a role in panic disorders.[15]

With all of this in mind, are antianxiety medications truly just a "crutch"? Consider this: a crutch can provide temporary help (example: someone with a broken leg), or it can be of permanent assistance (example: an individual born without a leg). In both cases, crutches meet a vital need. Similarly, psychotropic medications have an important role to play in a wide range of sufferers' circumstances.

During the time I had received the medication prescription but had resisted getting it filled, Diana pointed out something to me. "Randy, if you had heart disease, would you take medication for it?"

"Sure."

"What about cancer? Do you think modern science might have something to offer you?"

"Well, yeah."

"And if you happened to be diabetic, may I assume that you'd be open to receiving regular injections of insulin?"

"Yes." By now, of course, I could see that I'd already stepped with both feet into the trap set for me.

"Well, I just don't think this is any different. Just like you wouldn't be able to think your way out of heart disease, I don't believe you can think your way out of anxiety disorders."

Again, while I won't pretend to speak for others suffering from OCD, panic attacks, or agoraphobia, I believe Diana was right about my situation. The weight of evidence—both before and after medication—was too strong to suggest that I could simply believe my way to wellness. Yes, there were things I could do to help, such as finding a strong counselor to guide me in resolving lingering emotional issues. I made that call too, and over time it's helping me to unlock some deeply embedded factors that contributed to my overall anxiety picture. For me, medication combined with therapy packed a powerful, positive behavioral punch. Sometimes that's what dealing with hidden issues can feel like: a sucker punch. But after the pain and tears, I knew life would never be the same, and that was a very good thing.

The bottom line echoes what Elli Purtell stated previously, "There is no one-size-fits-all answer. The right remedy varies from person to person." It's up to each person to explore the options and make a decision based on what makes the most sense. That may involve experimenting with a variety of approaches until the right solution eventually surfaces. The good news is that today, relief is likely to present itself much sooner than some of us found it in the past. There is an ever-expanding bevy of medication options, including serotonin-norepinephrine reuptake inhibitors. SNRIs act in similar fashion to

SSRIs, but target a slightly different area of the brain. Whatever medication is chosen (and there are many), the latest research suggests that the combination of medication plus therapy provides the biggest recovery bang for your buck.

Our biochemical imbalances are not only shaped by genetics, but they are also shaped by our thoughts. Consider this from HuffingtonPost.com blogger Debbie Hampton: "Expectancies and learned associations have been shown to change brain chemistry and circuitry which results in real physiological and cognitive outcomes, such as less fatigue, lower immune system reaction, elevated hormone levels, and reduced anxiety. . . . You are speaking to your genes with every thought you have. The fast growing field of epigenetics is showing that who you are is the product of the things that happen to you in your life, which change the way your genes operate. Genes are actually switched on or off depending on your life experiences, and your genes and lifestyle form a feedback loop. Your life doesn't alter the genes you were born with. What changes is your genetic activity, meaning the hundreds of proteins, enzymes, and other chemicals that regulate your cells."[16]

In other words, we also have, to some degree, the power to control our chemistry. That's why research has shown that the most effective treatment for anxiety and depression is not medication alone, but a combination of medication or lifestyle changes and talk therapy. Talk therapy can make a lasting difference, but there also needs to be a biological-level intervention. For some people, that may mean medication, but it could also be accomplished through lifestyle changes or diet, depending on severity.

That's why it's important to consult with a doctor or psychiatrist.

Do I think anxiety disorders would resurface if I made a decision to stop my medication regime? In my case, I think it's likely, and research seems to back me up. I have, however, experimented with lowering the dosage. I could tell when I'd reached my minimum "threshold," and felt certain symptoms once again beginning to manifest themselves. I made the appropriate adjustment, and soon once again felt better.

Because the human brain is a delicate masterpiece of engineering, I do not write without great consideration when suggesting that altering its chemistry may hold benefits. While you should consult a doctor or physician before changing medications, the reality is that it's difficult to know what the long-term consequences are for certain medications.[17] Many of these medications were not designed for long-term use, which is why terms such as "temporary" and "weaning off" are still part of therapists' vocabulary. Nevertheless, I cannot bring myself to ignore suffering when relief might be close at hand. Sometimes that means reaching for a bottle or box of life-changing medication. It may not be magic, but it could be just what's needed to lift you out of the ditch and get you back on the road.

SEVENTEEN

YOU CAN RISE ABOVE ANXIETY

"Dear Mr. Fishell,
    Greetings from Colorado Springs, and many thanks for your recent letter. I value your words of support . . . and it was tremendously encouraging to learn that the Lord has allowed us to play such a pivotal role in your life."

The personal letter from Dr. James Dobson came in response to one I'd sent as editor of *Guide* magazine, the children's publication where I spent more than twenty-five years as an editor. I'd received word that Dr. Dobson had heard rumors that my denomination had played a role in perpetuating negative comments about a certain political stance that he'd supposedly taken. While I've not always agreed with every position he or certain other evangelical Christians have taken on a variety of issues, I tend to admire people who stand strong on their sincerely held convictions.

The issue at hand involved a rumor so ridiculous that I'd wasted no time in letting Dr. Dobson know that my publication had played no role in helping to perpetuate it. His closing comments were heartwarming: "The time you've taken to offer that clarification—along with your kind affirmation of me and the work of Focus—means a great deal to me."

But what I'd really wanted him to know was that it was on his radio program so many years earlier that I'd first learned that my condition had a name.

As I laid the letter down on my desk, my mind swirled. How was it possible that a letter from me meant "a great deal" to this man? After all, *I* was the broken individual, wasn't I? Wasn't it *I*, a struggling seminarian, who'd caught a glimpse of hope that dark night some three decades earlier as I jogged along a dark street listening to a radio broadcast hailing from the other side of the country? Though it would be a long time before I'd make life-changing progress, that broadcast featuring Dr. Dobson had served as a lifeline.

Now I think I understand why my letter meant so much to him. Even though he didn't really know me, my comments affirmed to Dr. Dobson that his work had made a difference to someone in real time and space. Maybe that's what drives healing professionals of every discipline: occasionally learning that their efforts have not been in vain.

The possibility of making a difference to someone is why it's been worth it for me to dredge up some painful memories in writing this book. More than once I felt anew the shame and despair that haunted me as I battled OCD, panic disorder, and agoraphobia. I'm not a healing professional, but rather, I consider myself a "wounded healer." I've been there, done that, and don't want *you* to experience one more day of unnecessary suffering.

Our lives are a puzzle, comprised of, among other things, physical, mental, social, and spiritual pieces. When one or more of those pieces suffer damage, it affects the whole picture. Today, scientific research has led to breathtaking discoveries and treatment options that bring new hope to once seemingly hopeless cases, including mental illness. A bevy of effective approaches to treating anxiety and its related disorders awaits those who choose to pursue a solution.

In 1974, the Grammy Award for Song of the Year went to Barbara Streisand for "The Way We Were," the theme song from the movie of the same name. Written by Alan Bergman, Marilyn Bergman, and Marvin Hamlisch, this wistful tune has won many other awards down through the years. The song captures and reflects the power and pain associated with human memory.

Memories can play an important role in both keeping anxiety alive and putting it behind you. For example, agoraphobia develops primarily due to the bad memory associated with panic episodes. If it happened to be while driving, you remember the horrible sensations that took place while on the road. I remember avoiding a certain pharmacy because I developed panic while in that store. Or perhaps a certain setting, such as a beach at sunset, evokes a strong memory of a romance gone wrong. Suddenly depression—"anger turned inward," as some therapists label it—descends like a thick cloud. Many different settings, people, and even thoughts, can stir up anxiety-producing memories.

Dr. Claire Weekes makes clear that such memories

are not entitled to claim victory. She begins by mentioning the despair so often associated with anxiety disorders.

You probably look at others in the street and wonder why you can't be like them. What is this "terrible thing" that has happened to you? What is the meaning of these terrible feelings?

Such feelings may have possessed you for a long time, even for years. Indeed, you may have reached a point of such desperate suffering that you could be thinking of ending it all, or may even have attempted to do just that. And yet, however deeply involved you may be in nervous illness, however long you may have suffered, you can recover and enjoy life again. I emphasize *however deeply involved and however long.* The main difference between a person ill for many years and someone ill for a short time is that the one who suffered for long has had more time to collect disturbing memories, especially the memory of much defeat, so that he despairs easily. But there is nothing altered within this person determining that because he has been ill for so long, he cannot possibly recover now.[1]

Memories can produce discomfort, but they are merely thoughts. They are not dangerous, they cannot force their will upon you. Richard Carlson writes, "Just as a check is worthless without your signature, your thoughts cannot harm you without your consent. You could be having the worst series of thoughts . . . but if you remember that they are just thoughts and nothing else, you will be able to dismiss them, or at the very least, to give them less significance."[2] Perhaps more important, once you begin rising above your anxiety disorders, new memories will form to replace many of those that helped to hold you back.

Along with sad or anxiety-producing memories, you may on occasion experience what is known as a "setback." This means that once in a while, you may sense that instead of progressing, you're regressing. When I was trying to beat anxiety with behavior modification alone, I experienced many setbacks. The truth is, virtually any setback will never take you back to where you started. In my case, I found that setbacks played very little role with my particular protocol: counseling and medication. Progress was rapid beyond anything I'd tried before.

Again, I'm not urging medication on anyone. My goal is to persuade you that whatever healing route you choose, you *can* rise above anxiety disorders. Don't let anyone—especially yourself—tell you differently. It's time to start making some new memories.

Albuquerque, New Mexico, is fairly stunning from the air at night. But then, so are Los Angeles, Orlando, Dallas, Chicago, and many other cities into which I've flown since regaining the ability to travel freely. (I won't say that I've *never* had a twinge of anxiety since those days, but it's been wonderful by comparison!)

I'm not sure if you're like me in this respect, but often on such occasions, I'll look out the airplane window at the shimmering city lights below and grow thoughtful. For me, thoughts such as these may rise to the surface: *How many people down there are suffering? Can I some-*

how make a difference to at least one or two of them?
Why did I find relief and not them?

Of course, not all suffering resembles the kind of mental anguish I've written about. Human suffering spans such a gamut that a complete listing would never be up to date. Although we celebrate new solutions and cures for some present maladies, suffering is continually reinventing itself. A primary task for me is opening a window of hope so that someone living in the clutches of an anxiety disorder might discover a new pathway to peace. That may or may not include medication, but I urge those suffering from anxiety as I once did to leave no treatment stone unturned.

Earlier, I spoke about the risks and benefits associated with all medications. Along with exercising caution when prescribing Paxil® to children and teens, the drug has been associated with a few other *possible* negative outcomes.[3] As I earlier implied, a lot of things we swallow *could* produce a bad reaction. It might even be that chicken salad sandwich you ate for lunch. The odds are (though not overly likely) that it contained e-coli, but still, there was a chance. I do not mean to belittle research findings strongly suggesting that some medications may elicit dangerous responses in certain individuals. Whether or not you decide to include medication as part of your recovery protocol, there is an even more important decision that I urge you to make: the decision to do *something* rather than nothing. Your life is a gift, and it is selfish to deprive others of your giftedness by giving in to anxiety.

I have not mentioned Paxil® in order to promote any particular medication. Indeed, paroxetine, the generic name for the drug, wasn't even originally indicated for the treatment of panic. Rather, Dr. Raj Kumar was later responsible for finding several new uses for the drug, including panic disorder, social-anxiety disorder, post-traumatic stress disorder, and obsessive-compulsive disorder.[4] So, again, I am in no way suggesting that Paxil® is necessarily right for you. Indeed, there are many other possibilities that your medical professional may consider as being more likely to succeed in your specific circumstances, including anxiolytic (anti-anxiety) medications.

I suffered a long time before finding a workable solution to my anxiety disorders. Despite all appearances to the contrary, something life-changing for me was in the works behind the scenes. Help was being formulated even though I had no such knowledge at the time. This is a powerful reminder that even when we think things will never change, a solution—*your* solution—may be in the works. As with so many medications, paroxetine and other SSRI and SNRI medications might well be superseded by something even more effective for anxiety disorders. For example, one research study involving rats concluded, "These findings provide the first evidence that the vasopressinergic system is likely to be critically involved in the behavioral and neuroendocrine effects of antidepressant drugs. This novel mechanism of action of paroxetine on vasopressin gene regulation renders vasopressinergic neuronal circuits a promising target for the development of more causal antidepressant treatment strategies."[5] That's a fancy way of saying that something new and exciting may be just around the corner.

Over the next few pages, I will share a few nuggets of hard-earned wisdom about recovering from obsessive-compulsive disorder, panic disorder, and agoraphobia. These comments should not be taken as a "secret formula" for overcoming such challenges. Rather, they are simply a few things that worked for me. Since I am not a psychiatrist or medical professional, view them as the reflections of a "seasoned amateur." My guess is that you'll find something worthy of consideration. Once again, there is no "one-size-fits-all" fix for obsessive-compulsive disorder, panic attacks, or agoraphobia. But there are common threads that tend to be woven throughout these and similar dysfunctions. In the section "A Few Healing Thoughts," see what resonates with you, and with the help of qualified professionals, begin weaving your own tapestry of healing. If you're crushed by the weight of anxiety, you will find your burden beginning to lighten. If panic has left your life in tatters, know that peace lies just around the corner. And if agoraphobia has imprisoned you, you can find freedom. But it won't happen on its own—it's up to you to make the call.

For many years, Krause's Corner stood on the corner of Ferry and Main Streets in Berrien Springs, my hometown. The building is still there, but it's not the same. Back when I was a kid, the drugstore featured a soda fountain, and they also developed film. (Yes, cameras used to have a long roll of plastic stuff inside them that had to be immersed in chemicals as part of the picture-making process. Incredible.)

One day after a visit to the doctor (I'd been ill with some childhood illness, but I can't remember the specific ailment), Mom pulled up in front of Krause's. She knew they had a spinning rack inside that held children's books. Inside, we walked up to the rack. "You can choose two books," Mom said. One of the books I chose featured a kid who could never seem to get the hang of doing life. Maybe I closely identified with Charlie Brown or something, but for whatever reason, that *Peanuts* book became a cherished and comforting part of my boyhood.

What I learned only recently is that the creative force behind *Peanuts*, the late Charles Schulz, knew something about anxiety disorders. In *My Life With Charlie Brown*, he wrote:

> Maybe the secret to not getting old is not to grow up. I'm not a completely grown-up, really. I find that I still feel out of place most of the time. At different times I've had trouble traveling and become almost agoraphobic. I'm always insecure. I think I'll always be an anxious person. Somebody asked me in an interview recently, "What are you anxious about?" I said, "If I knew, I wouldn't be anxious."[6]

Regarding his quest for excellence in rendering cartoon characters, he said:

> Sometimes I feel it is obsessive, like people who click their teeth and find that they have to do it in even numbers, or people who can't resist counting telephone poles. It may even be some kind of neurosis, but at least it accomplishes something for me.[7]

As a bit of a cartoonist myself, I take heart that maybe counting things and clicking my teeth isn't so bad after all. Maybe I'll create the next Linus or Snoopy—who knows?

More seriously, much as when I used to think that no one else on Planet Earth had ever experienced what I was enduring, so I reasoned that nobody clicked their teeth and counted things to make it through the day. It turns out that at least a few others know what I'm talking about. And maybe, just maybe, there are even more—perhaps millions, who know the anguish and exhaustion that come from battling anxiety disorders that go by different names. Such comforting knowledge alone can't "fix" us, but somehow it helps to know that we're not alone. We can learn together and lift each other up, in person, on-line, in healing groups, and in so many other ways. It all starts with embracing the reality that humanity is flawed. Ending the shame and stigma associated with mental ill-ness should become a priority, not only for society, but also for us individually. As we do, we achieve the status of "wounded healers"—damaged yet recovering persons on a mission to bring hope to others. I increasingly ap-preciate the perspective that Charles Schulz shared ear-lier in his career: "Recently I published a little series of cartoons on the subject of security. . . . Linus is kneeling with his arms on his bed, and the caption reads, 'Security is knowing you are not alone.'"[8]

If you're battling an anxiety disorder, you're not alone. I bid you Godspeed on your journey of recovery. Or per-haps it's a friend, relative, or work colleague whose life has been impacted by some form of anxiety. Share this book and urge them to choose to do whatever it takes to recover the joy that is so abundant when we are able to rise above an anxious kind of mind.

APPENDICES

APPENDIX A

A Few Healing Thoughts

You may have noticed that the subtitle of this book contains the phrase "rising above" and not "victory over." Yes, I'm doing really well these days. But I still deal with the fallout that comes with being human. In my case, as you've read, this involves several strata on the anxiety disorders spectrum. So while I cannot promise a permanent cure, I *can* tell you that anxiety disorders do not have to block the way to achieving your hopes and dreams. In addition to what you may have already chosen to adopt from reading about my journey, here are a few more thoughts and strategies that I've found helpful.

Accept the hand you've been dealt. There is nothing to be gained by wishing you'd been born different. Whatever your anxiety disorder, use the struggle as a gift, a heaven-sent opportunity to become the real you. Rather than fight the person you are, use the knowledge you've accumulated and will continue to accumulate to grow into a more fulfilled and empowered version of you.

Take a risk and do *something*. Today there are many individual and group resources available to help you rise above anxiety and other mental disorders. Although I strongly recommend that you initially get evaluated by a qualified psychiatrist, you can also find help from other healing professionals. This includes your family physician, clinical psychologists, licensed clinical social workers, and others. Unless you're really OK living with a crippling anxiety disorder, staying where you're at should not be an option. More than likely, at some point you'll simply need to take a well-reasoned leap of faith. For me, that involved swallowing a pill. It was a difficult choice, but I will never forget the emphasis my psychiatrist placed on the relief of suffering. Do yourself and others a favor by researching effective and affordable treatment options, then just do it.

Bear in mind that any effective therapy will take some time, and the most lasting progress typically results from a multifaceted treatment plan, such as medication plus a psychotherapy option. In my own case, this type of protocol—a combination of talk therapy and medication—resulted in progress happening much faster than I'd anticipated. It may happen the same way for you. (From my vantage point, I cannot imagine anyone that could not benefit from some form of counseling, mental illness or not.)

Ditch the shame. Like so many who struggle with mental health, you may be awash in shame. *Beat it down without mercy*. If you're part of the human race, you've got issues—period. These may involve physical, emotional, or relational challenges—the list is endless. You simply cannot continue to endure shame just because your issue involves your thought processes. You probably don't look down on a girl whose fall from a horse left her a paraplegic. I trust that you don't think less of an elderly gentleman because he has to lug an oxygen tank around behind him in order to survive. We're all in this together, and none of us has the right to shame another or ourselves.

Tap into the power of purpose. It may sound strange, but I attribute my recovery success in part to the fact that I felt called to become a magazine editor. I simply didn't have enough mental space left to devote full-time to anxiety. Instead, I was constantly being consumed by the daily grind so typical of the publishing industry. So what's *your* passion? How much fuller could your professional life be without the constant drag of anxiety? Don't have a passion? Make finding one your passion! That pursuit alone will prove more energizing than you realize. It can be a first step toward a much more rewarding future. Just don't use busyness as an excuse to avoid dealing with your mental health challenge(s).

Do not neglect the spiritual side of healing. Humans are deeply spiritual beings, and we cannot separate ourselves into separate components. The mind-body connection is very real, and this includes our spiritual selves. Recently, a therapist reminded me of how important spirituality can be when dealing with anxiety. He pointed out that at the core of such fears resides a fear of death or even hell. Our spiritual beliefs play an important part in our recovery, for good or for bad. That's why you may want to consider looking at them more closely if they cause you anxiety.

Keep reading, learning, and sharing. Whether it's on a screen or in print, never stop expanding your knowledge about what challenges you. The more you know, the more you grow. In a forum of your choosing, share where you've been and what's working in moving you to a better place. Your story may be exactly what someone suffering needs to hear.

APPENDIX B

Support Tips

There are several possible reactions from others once they find out that you're battling an anxiety disorder. Here are a few common responses.

▶ **"It's all in your head—get over it."** By now you know that this is both simplistic and simply untrue. The mind-body connection is far too integrated for such an appraisal and is usually dispensed by someone who's uninformed about the pertinent issues.

▶ **"I really can't relate, so it's probably best for me not to get involved."** It can be hard to see a loved one, friend, coworker or other individual not make an effort to further understand your situation. They may even think you're "crazy" and maintain some distance from you. If this happens, try to realize that similar to the first situation, it's the other person's lack of information that's the core issue, not your condition. Personally, I've found the vast majority of people I'm close to with whom I shared my condition fell into the next category.

▶ **"I may not fully understand what you're going through, but we've all got issues. How can I help?"** These are the individuals who understand the nature of the human condition, and you should care for them as much as they care for you. What follows I write directly to them.

▶ **Read this book cover to cover.** When you've finished, you should have a much better understanding of what people who battle anxiety disorders go through. Yes, it is a mental illness, but we are not "crazy." The first step toward real support is to begin understanding.

▶ **Don't automatically assume a posture of "tough love" or push us too hard too fast.** Recovering from an anxiety disorder can be different than other recovery protocols. Beyond that, every person is unique and will need room to both succeed and fail. Pushing too hard can bring more failure than success. A good support person is more like a coach, talking through issues as needed, asking good questions, and giving ample affirmation and encouragement after each success. As a support person, you'll experience some frustration that things may not be going as quickly as you anticipated. Guess what—you won't be as frustrated as the person you're supporting. True, if recovery comes to a standstill, a few words of gentle encouragement may be appropriate. But don't overdo it. Recovery can seem more like crossing an ocean, not a creek.

▶ **Don't push a particular recovery protocol.** Instead, help the person recovering gather as much information as necessary. (See Appendix C.) If you're a close friend or loved one, it may be appropriate to assist the person in deciding which steps to take first, such as a referral from a family physician to a psychiatrist (who can prescribe medication), a clinical psychologist, or other specialist. Medication may or may not be part of the protocol. Leave the initial evaluations to the specialists, and go from there.

▶ **Exercise great patience.** This may be the most important—and most challenging—role that you play. It can be very easy to grow frustrated with something you don't fully understand. Try to think of something you experience that's an issue for you. Do you relish patience as you try to deal with problems? Try to lavishly extend grace, hope, and encouragement rather than question why things aren't going the way you wish.

▶ **Participate in the recovery process as appropriate.** This may mean driving someone to appointments or other recovery-related meetings, taking part in an exercise program with the recovering person, helping to ensure that medications are regularly taken, and other meaningful gestures.

▶ **If you are a praying person, ramp it up.** Assuming you've read this book, you know that its author is a person of faith and believes that God can bring an added dimension to the healing process. Employ the tools of faith at your disposal.

APPENDIX C

Treatment Methods

According to the National Institutes of Mental Health, "Anxiety disorders are generally treated with psychotherapy, medication, or both." Following are several current anxiety disorder treatment methods and their explanations from their website.

▸ **Psychotherapy.** Psychotherapy or "talk therapy" . . . must be directed at the person's specific anxieties and tailored to his or her needs. A typical "side effect" of psychotherapy is temporary discomfort involved with thinking about confronting feared situations.

▸ **Cognitive Behavioral Therapy (CBT).** CBT . . . teaches a person different ways of thinking, behaving, and reacting to anxiety-producing and fearful situations. CBT can also help people learn and practice social skills, which is vital for treating social anxiety disorder.

Two specific stand-alone components of CBT used to treat social anxiety disorder are **cognitive therapy** and **exposure therapy**. Cognitive therapy focuses on identifying, challenging, and then neutralizing unhelpful thoughts underlying anxiety disorders. Exposure therapy focuses on confronting the fears underlying an anxiety disorder in order to help people engage in activities they have been avoiding. Exposure therapy is used along with relaxation exercises and/or imagery. Both have much research showing effectiveness.

▸ While CBT has been shown to be effective in treating anxiety, other forms of therapy can work, as well. For those who have difficulty controlling their thoughts, an emphasis on acceptance and exploration may be helpful. There are many **other therapies** as well, such as dialectical behavioral therapy (DBT), acceptance and commitment therapy (ACT), Gestalt therapy, and emotion-focused therapy (EFT). "Research shows that the most effective treatment is a combination of medication plus talk therapy, not either alone," comments Dr. Thomas Luttrell, a therapist who works with anxiety in the context of relationships. Regarding his view of effective therapy for anxiety, he states, "I believe it involves acceptance and resolving shame around the disorder, as well as unpacking worst-case scenarios with the purpose of having greater awareness about our fears and learning how to cope with those fears, *not* for the purpose of trying to stop thoughts or encouraging more avoidance."

▸ **Self-help or support groups.** Some people with anxiety disorders might benefit from joining a self-help or support group and sharing their problems and achievements with others. Internet chat rooms might also be useful, but any advice received over the Internet should be used with caution, as Internet acquaintances have usually never seen each other, and false identities are common. Talking with a trusted friend or member of the clergy can also provide support, but it is not necessarily a sufficient alternative to care from an expert clinician.

▸ **Stress-management techniques.** Stress management techniques and meditation can help people with anxiety disorders calm themselves and may enhance the effects of therapy. While there is evidence that aerobic exercise has a calming effect, the quality of the studies is not strong enough to support its use as treatment. Since caffeine, certain illicit drugs, and even some over-the-counter cold medications can aggravate the symptoms of anxiety disorders, avoiding them should be considered. Check with your physician or pharmacist before taking any additional medications.

▸ **Medication.** Medication does not cure anxiety disorders but often relieves symptoms. Medication can only be prescribed by a medical doctor (such as a psychiatrist or a primary care provider), but a few states allow psychologists to prescribe psychiatric medications.

Medications are sometimes used as the initial treatment of an anxiety disorder, or are used only if there is insufficient response to a course of psychotherapy. As has been repeatedly stated in this book, research has shown that patients treated with a combination of psychotherapy and medication typically have better outcomes than those treated with only one or the other.

The most common classes of medications used to combat anxiety disorders are antidepressants, anti-anxiety drugs, and beta-blockers. Be aware that some medications are effective only if they are taken regularly and that symptoms may recur if the medication is stopped.

Including medication as part of your recovery protocol is a very personal decision. Some may have great reserves of willpower to face their fears without biochemical assistance and come out the other side victorious. If that description seems likely to fit your situation, then go for it. But for others, including those suffering from depression, I encourage you to do adequate research on the current findings regarding likely physiological factors involved in your particular disorder. It may be that the right drug will provide the missing element needed to rebalance your body's chemistry and help you to reclaim a life of joy.

Learn more at https://www.nimh.nih.gov/health/topics/anxiety-disorders/index.shtml.

APPENDIX D

A Few Helpful Resources

Websites

▶ **National Institutes of Mental Health**

Helpful general information on anxiety disorders.

http://www.nimh.nih.gov/health/topics/anxiety-disorders/index.shtml

▶ **International OCD Foundation**

https://iocdf.org/

▶ **Anxiety and Depression Association of America**

http://www.adaa.org/understanding-anxiety/obsessive-compulsive-disorder-ocd

▶ **National Alliance on Mental Illness**

https://www.nami.org/

On Panic Disorder and Agoraphobia

http://www.adaa.org/understanding-anxiety/panic-disorder-agoraphobia

▶ **Panic Disorder Self-Screening Test**

http://www.adaa.org/screening-panic-disorder

▶ **Anxiety and Depression Association of**

America podcasts

Podcasts on a wide range of anxiety disorders.

http://www.adaa.org/podcasts-ask-learn

Recommended Reading:

Healing the Child Within, by Dr. Charles Whitfield (recovering from a dysfunctional family)

OCD: A Guide for the Newly Diagnosed, by Dr. Michael A. Tompkins, Ph.D. (OCD)

Peace From Nervous Suffering, by Dr. Claire Weekes (agoraphobia and panic)

The Highly Sensitive Person, by Dr. Elaine Aron (physical and emotional sensitivity)

The Man Who Couldn't Stop, by David Adam (OCD)

NOTES

Chapter 1: Panic on the South Side

1. http://en.wikipedia.org/wiki/Panic. Accessed December 7, 2014.

2. http://www.psybersquare.com/anxiety/ panic_biochem.html. Accessed June 9, 2017.

3. Google search term: etymology of panic. Accessed January 8, 2015.

4. http://en.wikipedia.org/wiki/Panic. Accessed January 8, 2015.

Chapter 2: Over and Over Again

1. Gary L. Wenk, *Your Brain on Food* (Bethesda, MD: Oxford University Press, 2010, 2015), 92.

Chapter 3: Steps in the Wrong Direction

1. http://www.disabled-world.com/artman/ publish/famous-ocd.shtml/. Accessed February 12, 2015.

2. http://www.nursingschools.net/ blog/2010/10/50-famous-successful-people-with-ocd/. Accessed February 12, 2015.

3. Ibid.

4. www.dailymail.co.uk/femail/article-1217283/
The-curse-OCD-It-latest-trendy-celebrity-
affliction-stories-prove-Obsessive-
Compulsive-Disorder-wrecks-lives.html.
Accessed February 12, 2015

5. http://www.disabled-world.com/artman/
publish/famous-ocd.shtml/. Accessed February
12, 2015.

6. http://www.google.com. Accessed February 12,
2015.

7. http://www.psychiatrictimes.com/
obsessive-compulsive-disorder/expert-
insights-obsessive-compulsive-disorder. This web
page also contains a helpful video in which Dr.
Simpson provides helpful insight regarding obsessive-compulsive disorder.

8. Ibid.

9. David Adam, *The Man Who Couldn't Stop* (New
York, NY: Sarah Crichton Books/Farrar, Straus, and
Giroux, 2014), 259.

10. Scriptures credited to NIV are taken from THE
HOLY BIBLE, NEW INTERNATIONAL VERSION®,
NIV®. Copyright © 1973, 1978, 1984, 2011 by
Biblica, Inc.® Used by permission. All rights re-
served worldwide.

11. http://en.wikipedia.org/wiki/Chuck_Hughes.
Accessed on March 3, 2015.

Chapter 4: Heavenly Dysfunction

1. https://www.mentalhealth.gov/basics/myths-facts/. Accessed July 19, 2016.

2. https://www.sciencedaily.com/releases/2006/10/061024010331.htm. Accessed on June 9, 2017.

3. *AARP Bulletin*, March, 2017, 38.

4. Ibid.

5. http://www.psychiatrictimes.com/articles/religion-spirituality-and-mental-health. Accessed on March 6, 2015.

6. Ibid.

7. Ibid.

8. Ibid.

9. J. B. Phillips, *Your God Is Too Small* (New York, NY: Simon & Schuster, 1952, 1998 by Vera May Phillips), 30, 31.

10. David Adam, *The Man Who Couldn't Stop* (New York, NY: Sarah Crichton Books/Farrar, Strauss, and Giroux, 2014), 118.

11. Ibid., 119.

12. Ibid., 117.

Chapter 7: Arresting Events

1. David Adam, *The Man Who Couldn't Stop* (New York, NY: Sarah Crichton Books/Farrar, Straus, and Giroux, 2014), 15.

2. Ibid., 16.

3. Bob Elliott and Ray Goulding, *Write If You Get Work: The Best of Bob and Ray* (New York: Random House, 1975), 70.

4. *Bob Montgomery, Ph.D. and Laurel Morris, Ph.D., Living With Anxiety* (Boston, MA: Da Capo Life-Long/Pereus Books Group, 1992) 2, 3.

5. Ibid., 3, 4.

6. https://opinionator.blogs.nytimes.com/2012/09/22/america-the-anxious/?mcubz=0&_r=0. Accessed on June 9, 2017.

Chapter 8: Short-Bus Homies

1. http://www.md-health.com/Heart-Skipping-Beats-Frequently.html. Accessed May 21, 2015.

2. https://www.psychologytoday.com/blog/anxiety-files/201007/why-thought-stopping-doesn-t-work

Chapter 9: Muhammad Ali's Wife and the Mattress

1. http://www.nursingdegreeguide.org/2010/100-weird-phobias-that-really-exist/. Accessed May 26, 2015.

2. This is another story in itself. I personally went along on the mattress delivery to the Ali home. Try as we might, the driver and I simply could not squeeze the new mattress up through the home's narrow staircase. We knew it could be done, because someone had gotten the old mattress out! Finally, a handyman who'd been working outside painting asked if he could try his hand at solving the mattress challenge. With a mighty heave he thrust the mattress upward and it popped onto the second story floor. Somehow, the second piece of the set followed suit. My ego suffered significant damage.

3. https://www.psychologytoday.com/blog/sense-and-sensitivity/201210/coping-anxiety-hsp. Accessed June 4, 2015.

Chapter 10: "It" Has a Name

1. Today there is a brick bearing my name in the sidewalk near Seminary Hall. Such bricks were placed to honor donors who'd provided funds to enlarge the building. I never gave anything, but my parents did. Instead of having their own names

engraved in the brick, they put mine there, along with my wife's name. This may have been their attempt to alert the world that their ne'er-do-well son had actually gotten his life straightened out and married a fine woman.

2. https://www.psychologytoday.com/conditions/agoraphobia. Accessed on June 4, 2015.

3. Brant Hansen, *Unoffendable* (Nashville, TN: W Publishing Group/Thomas Nelson Publishers, 2015), 106, 107, quoting from Robert Sapolsky, *Why Zebras Don't Get Ulcers* (New York: Henry Holt, 2004).

4. Claire Weekes, *Peace From Nervous Suffering* (New York, NY: Penguin Group, 1972), 9.

5. Ibid., 18.

6. Ibid., 20.

7. Ibid., 5.

8. Ibid., 26.

9. Ibid., 27.

10. Ibid., 66.

11. Ibid., 23.

12. http://psychologytoday.psychtests.com/articles/mentalhealth/pd_brain.html. Accessed on December 29, 2015.

13. Elaine N. Aron, Ph.D., *The Highly-Sensitive Person* (New York, NY: Broadway Books, 1996), 28.

14. Ibid.

15. David Adam, *The Man Who Couldn't Stop* (New York, NY: Sarah Crichton Books/Farrar, Straus, and Giroux, 2014), 177.

Chapter 11: The Worst Vacation Ever

1. Quoted in Kathy Freston, *Veganist* (New York, NY: Hachette Books, 2011), 26.

2. *Emotional Agility* by Susan David, PhD, (New York, NY: Avery/Penguin Random House, copyright © 2016 by Susan David), 45.

3. Ibid., 47.

4. Ibid., 47, 48.

5. Ibid., 48.

6. Ibid., 48.

7. Ibid., 48.

8. http://www.mayoclinic.org/diseases-conditions/ depersonalization-derealization-disorder/symptoms-causes/dxc-20318902. Accessed on June 9, 2017.

Chapter 13: Hope Across the Bridge

1. Michael A. Tompkins, Ph.D., *OCD: A Guide for the Newly Diagnosed* (Oakland, CA: New Harbinger

Publications, Inc., 2012), 3.

2. Ibid., 3, 4.

3. http://anxietyandpanic.com/about.php. Accessed September 17, 2015.

4. http://www.nytimes.com/1991/10/31/us/arthur-b-hardy-78-psychiatrist-who-treated-a-fear-of-going-out.html. Accessed September 23, 2015.

Chapter 14: On the Move

1. David McRaney, *You Are Not So Smart* (New York, NY: Penguin Group, 2011), 163.

2. Ibid., 162.

3. Ibid., 163.

4. R. Davidhiszar, abstract: "The Pursuit of Illness for Secondary Gain": http://www.ncbi.nlm.nih.gov/pubmed/10172109. Accessed May 2, 2016.

5. Adapted from Alice Boyles, series: "What Keeps People From Solving Their Problems": http://www.aliceboyes.com/secondary-gain/ Accessed May 2, 2016.

6. https://en.wikipedia.org/wiki/Impostor_syndrome. Accessed May 31, 2016.

7. http://www.nytimes.com/2007/07/24/health/psychology/24fear.html?pagewanted=all&_r=0

Chapter 16: "I Think I Can Help You"

1. http://www.theguardian.com/society/2002/apr/28/mentalhealth1. Accessed on December 13, 2015.

2. Ibid.

3. http://www.mayoclinic.org/diseases-conditions/depression/in-depth/ssris/art-20044825. Accessed on June 9, 2017.

4. Ibid.

5. https://www.nami.org/Learn-More/Treatment/Mental-Health-Medications/Paroxetine-%28Paxil%29. Accessed on December 22, 2015.

6. http://www.briancollinson.ca/index.php/2012/11/jungian-therapy-and-the-meaning-of-dreams-houses.html. Accessed on December 22, 2015.

7. http://www.huffingtonpost.com/elli-purtell/why-i-chose-anti-anxiety-medication_b_7130254.html. Accessed on December 28, 2015.

8. Ibid.

9. Ibid.

10. http://www.nhs.uk/conditions/SSRIs-%28selective-serotonin-reuptake-inhibitors%29/Pages/Introduction.aspx. Accessed on December 28, 2015.

11. Ibid.

12. http://www.nimh.nih.gov/news/science-news/2009/runaway-vigilance-hormone-linked-to-panic-attacks.shtml. Accessed on December 28, 2015.

13. https://www.bbrfoundation.org/content/to-day%E2%80%99s-new-york-times-reports-discovery-about-brain%E2%80%99s-fearpanic-response. Accessed on June 9, 2017.

14. Barbara Strauch, *The Secret Life of the Grown-Up Brain* by Barbara Strauch (New York, NY: Viking/Penguin Group, 2010), 31.

15. https://www.bbrfoundation.org/content/today%E2%80%99s-new-york-times-reports-discovery-about-brain%E2%80%99s-fearpanic-response. Accessed on June 9, 2017.

16. http://www.huffingtonpost.com/debbie-hampton/how-your-thoughts-change-your-brain-cells-and-genes_b_9516176.html

17. See http://www.psy-world.com/SSRI_problems.pdf and http://www.huffingtonpost.com/dr-peter-breggin/antidepressants-long-term-depression_b_1077185.html

Chapter 17: You Can Rise Above Anxiety Disorders

1. Claire Weekes, *Hope and Help for Your Nerves* (New York, NY: New American Library, a division

of Penguin Putnam Inc., 1969), 2.

2. Richard Carlson, Ph.D, *Easier Than You Think* (San Francisco, CA: HarperSanFrancisco [Harper One], 2005), 17.

3. http://articles.latimes.com/2014/feb/18/ science/la-sci-sn-antidepressant-paxil-breast-cancer-20140218. Accessed December 28, 2015.

4. http://www.theguardian.com/society/2002/ apr/28/mentalhealth1. Accessed on December 15, 2015.

5. http://www.nature.com/npp/journal/v28/n2/ full/1300040a.html. Accessed on December 29, 2015.

6. Charles M. Schulz, *My Life With Charlie Brown* (Jackson, MS: University Press of Mississippi, 2010 by Schulz Family Intellectual Property), 65.

7. Ibid., 101.

8. Ibid., 25.

Stay in touch with Randy Fishell

www.AnAnxiousKindofMind.com
www.Facebook.com/AnAnxiousKindofMind

CPSIA information can be obtained
at www.ICGtesting.com
Printed in the USA
LVOW08s0723201217
560362LV00006B/1859/P